A love letter to Kyoto
from the noma team

PHOTO: MITSURU WAKABAYASHI

NOMA IN KYOTO

10
CONTRIBUTORS
The noma team members and friends
who tell the stories of Noma in Kyoto

12
INTRODUCTION
Where it all started, where we ended up,
and how we got to Kyoto

16
HISTORY
How the imperial capital
developed its unique cuisine

22
LIQUID LIFE
Deep beneath the city lies the source of cuisine,
culture, and life itself

24
OMOTENASHI
The reason hospitality in Japan
goes above and beyond

28
MASTER OF IMAGINATION
Master Chef Yoshihiro Murata
on tradition and the future

36
A PERSON OF TWO CULTURES
The experience of Japan, when you are
born Japanese and a Westerner

38
CYCLE OF SEASONS
The Japanese year is divided into
72 different microseasons

46
THE STORY OF NOMA KYOTO IN 20 SERVINGS
The research, imagination, and creative process
of producing an entirely new menu

68
THE WAY OF FERMENTATION
On how fermentation is Japanese cuisine

72
CUTTING EDGE
Perhaps the best knives in the world

80
SOMMELIER JOURNEY
One woman's road trip in search of wine, sake,
and beer for a yet-to-be created menu

92
NIPPON NATURAL WINE CULTURE
The perspective of a person at the forefront
of the natural wine movement in Japan

94
SERVING TEA IN JAPAN
How to source something new and significant
in the home of the tea ceremony

PHOTO: BEN RICHARDS

Gion District

Low-rise neighborhoods of timber machiya houses remain along with ryokans and tea houses.

NOMA IN KYOTO

104
A LETTER FROM A LOCAL TEA FARMER

106
THE ART OF THE TABLE
Tableware that embodies old and new,
Japan and Denmark

116
HIDDEN TREASURES AND FLEA MARKETS
Where to find that certain something,
that burnished treasure for noma ambience

118
INTERIORS
The natural world and traditional crafts
created the design of Noma in Kyoto

122
BEYOND THE VEIL
The art of the tantalizing curtains
that screen the entrances of Japan

126
INSPIRED ENTRY
Noren and design from the brush of a 101-year-old master

134
COFFEE RITUAL
Of course, attention to detail is lavished
on every aspect of coffee

140
CERAMICS IN JAPAN
Kiln and kitchen meet in the ceramic arts

144
IZAKAYA CULTURE
Food, drink, and camaraderie:
welcome to your local

148
SAKE FOR BEGINNERS
Your guide to the world of the most
quintessential of Japanese drinks

150
DOS AND DON'TS
Manners, customs, and consideration of others
are important. Above all else: be polite

152
HIKE THROUGH HISTORY
Take a walk through culture and the past
in Kyoto's surrounding mountains

160
THE KYOTO GUIDE
The noma team shares where to eat and drink,
where to stay, and what to see

208
12 WEEKS IN KYOTO
Team noma during their three months in Kyoto

218
THANK YOU KYOTO
A poetic tribute to a memorable interlude

222
DIRECTORY
Where to find the best of Kyoto

NOMA IN KYOTO

PUBLISHER
noma

EDITORAL DIRECTOR
Nate French

EDITORIAL AND CREATIVE DIRECTION
noma, Ark Journal

GRAPHIC DESIGN
NR2154, Ian Bennett

RETOUCH
Werkstette, Flemming Roland, The Color Club

THANKS TO ALL CONTRIBUTORS
René Redzepi, Ditte Isager, Line Blomqvist, Fritz Buziek, Mitsuru Wakabayashi, Ichi Nakamura, Minechika Aidan, Ben Richards, Maria Cobo, Nate French, Traci Page Morris, Cory Smith, Ava Mees List, Carolyne Lane, Miko Klages, Craig Mod, Pablo Soto, Sara Aiko, Curated Kyoto, Amy Tang, Maiko Fukui, Discover Japan, POJ Studio, Folk Art Museum, Taro Hirano, Weekenders, Keisui Suzuki, OEO Studio, Yuki Hatta, Toru Miyaki, Paula Troxler, Kotaro Chiba, Ashlee Gillespie, U Yoshioka, Yougai, Kenneth Foong, Mario (Yusheng) Fu, Kevin Jeung, Risa Kamio, Miko Klages, Carolyne Lane, Nadine Levy Redzepi, Masanobu Egami, Kenichi Igawa, Samiro Yunoki, Yoshihiro Murata, Toryo Ito, Christine Rudolph, Gabe Ulla, Lily Collins, Shui Ishizaka, Margaret Lam, Thomas Lykke, Craig Mod, Aya Okamura, Robbie Swinnerton, Adam Sachs, Joji Sakurai, Robert Yellin, Lauren Hadler, Momoko Nakamura, Holly Anderson, Kyoto City Tourism Association, William Fraser, The noma team

COVER
Ashlee Jenna Gillespie (front) David Shrigley (back)

PUBLICATION DATE
November 2023

DISTRIBUTION
For sales and distribution enquiries, please email: contact@noma.dk

PRINTING
By Wind, Sweden

ISBN
978-87-974890-1-7

PAPER
Printed on arctic paper.
Munken Polar, Munken Print, Invercote G

TYPE
Freight Display, Neue Haas Grotesk

CONTACT
noma@noma.dk

All rights reserved.
No part of this publication may be reproduced, distributed or transmitted in any form or by any means, including photocopying or other electronic or mechanical methods, without prior written permission of the publisher, except in the case of brief quotations embodied in critical reviews and certain other noncommercial uses permitted by copyright law.
To request permission, write to: noma@noma.dk

Life goes on in the city that has robustly accommodated generations of change.

CONTRIBUTORS / NOMA

KENNETH FOONG

Hailing from Singapore, Kenneth Foong moved to New York to study Culinary Arts and Management and found his way into the halls of Eleven Madison Park and Betony before moving back to Restaurant Andre in Singapore. His journey with noma began in October 2018 as an intern and then as chef de partie, before taking over as head chef in June 2020. When not in kitchens, Kenneth enjoys time with his dog and swimming, biking, and running.

RISA KAMIO

Japanese-born Risa Kamio has lived in Denmark for almost 20 years. She started at noma in 2015 as the CEO's personal assistant, connecting Japan and noma at many levels, including working on the opening of Inua in Tokyo. For the Noma Kyoto pop-up, she was responsible for all coordination with Japan except for ingredients, arranging everything from visas and housing, to sourcing handmade tableware.

AVA MEES LIST

New York-born and Amsterdam-bred, head sommelier Ava Mees List arrived at noma in early 2019 after working in Paris for several years. She has a degree in cultural anthropology from the University of Amsterdam and a doctorate in waiting tables from the School of Hard Knocks. She lives among myriad books, paintings and flowers, as well as an impressive collection of vintage cashmere sweaters that urgently need mending. Ava Mees List goes by her middle name, pronounced Mase, or メイス.

NATE FRENCH

Born in Boston, Massachusetts, Nate French grew up with a big love for making music and exploring the world. He started cooking at a small restaurant north of Boston as a university summer job, and after completing political science studies and a circuitous journey, Nate landed in Copenhagen and worked his way up from an intern at noma to a sous chef in the test kitchen. His current role is assistant general manager, and he is working on an MBA.

MIKO KLAGES

Born in Cape Town, South Africa, from an early age Miko Klages could be found clinging to a rock face or his surfboard. His Bavarian mother tamed his mischievous nature. Via Switzerland, the Netherlands and South Korea, he made his way to Scandinavia, joining noma as a waiter. When he's not working, you can find him in Copenhagen, likely with a glass in one hand and a book in the other.

CHRISTINE RUDOLPH

For more than 20 years Christine Rudolph has worked as a freelance stylist. Copenhagen-based, she has lived in Australia and New York. In 2007 she styled the noma cookbook *Time and Place in Nordic Cuisine*. These days she is at noma each week doing the flowers and other tasks such as sourcing tableware and orchestrating seasonal decorations. She loves sun-ripened tomatoes, chilli, being in nature, forgetting to brush her hair–and her Blundstones.

MARIO (YUSHENG) FU

Exploring the boundaries and limits of food, seeking innovation through curiosity and creativity, is how Mario describes his journey. After studying food science and culinary art at the Basque Culinary Center in San Sebastián, Spain, Mario Fu interned in Restaurant Frantzén in Stockholm, worked at Restaurant Abac in Barcelona and then as researcher and R&D chef in Inua, Tokyo. During covid he worked as a food consultant in China. Since 2020, he has headed research in noma's fermentation lab.

CAROLYNE LANE

It was during a semester abroad in Germany that Carolyne Lane, originally from the UK, got her first restaurant job, pouring wines. Her curiosity for food and beverage grew and she dropped out of university to learn all she could, working for farms, coffee roasters and winemakers among others. Noma started off as a place to test a wide range of interests and see where she would land. Five years on, she has found her natural home as head of the tea and coffee program.

KEVIN JEUNG

Born and raised in Toronto, Canada, Kevin Jeung started as an intern at noma in 2015, helping to set up the original fermentation lab with Lars Wiliams and Arielle Johnson. After a stint in Toronto as pastry chef at Alo Restaurant, in 2019, he returned to noma to the fermentation lab. Since then, he has rotated through the service kitchen, been the forager and completed the circle by returning to the fermentation lab.

NADINE LEVY REDZEPI

Starting as an extra front-of-house while finishing school in 2005, Nadine Levy Redzepi fell completely in love with noma and started fulltime the following summer. In between having three daughters she managed all the bookings. In 2017 she wrote a cookbook *Downtime*, and now works on various projects, including pop-ups such as Kyoto. Outside work, she loves to cook, sew and spend as much time as possible with the girls.

CONTRIBUTORS / EXTERNAL

LILY COLLINS

Actress, author, philanthropist, and producer, Lily Collins is best known as the titular star in Netflix's *Emily in Paris*. Previous credits include *Extremely Wicked, Shockingly Evil And Vile, Rules Don't Apply, Mank*, among others. In 2022, she launched production company Case Study Films, alongside Charlie McDowell and Alex Orlovsky, to tell compelling and outside-of-the-box stories through a commercial lens. Its mission is to discover, nourish, and give voice to the next generation of storytellers.

MARGARET LAM

A food lover who finds the world too big and herself too little, Margaret Lam is always travelling for food experiences to broaden her universe. She fell in love with Japan decades ago and decided to move there temporarily, but that turned into a never-ending journey of learning as she continues to be mind-blown by the tiniest details Japanese people manage to perfect and take to the next level.

ROBBIE SWINNERTON

British food writer Robbie Swinnerton has lived and worked in Japan for more than 40 years. Based outside Tokyo in the historic coastal town of Kamakura, he continues to chart the dining scene in the metropolis through his restaurant review column, Tokyo Food File, which has run in *The Japan Times* newspaper since 1998. He has dined at noma in Copenhagen several times over the past 10 years, as well as at noma's pop-ups in Tokyo (2016) and Kyoto (2023).

MASANOBU EGAMI

In 2006, Masanobu Egami started Ethelvine in Kyoto as a small natural wine agent, first selling to restaurants and bars but soon also to many private customers. Over the years, the shop has grown into a national institution, often welcoming winemakers from all over the world for tastings. In 2018 he opened Dupree, a restaurant around the corner from Ethelvine, named after the legendary rhythm and blues guitarist Cornell Dupree. In fact, Egami is quite the gifted blues guitarist himself!

THOMAS LYKKE

After working at *Wallpaper* magazine, Thomas Lykke co-founded OEO Studio, a multidisciplinary design firm based in Copenhagen, that blends craftsmanship, sustainability and storytelling. He has worked with fashion houses, luxury hotels and high-end restaurants, using the concept of "narrative design" on projects to tell compelling stories and evoke an emotional response. He believes in the power of architecture and design to shape human experiences.

ADAM SACHS

New York-based food, travel and lifestyle writer, editor, consultant, occasional podcaster and committed (if wholly untrained) tinkerer in the kitchen, Adam Sachs is the recipient of three James Beard journalism awards. He has served as editor-in-chief of *Saveur* magazine, is a contributor to many magazines and is the director of S.A.L.T., a culinary program for Silversea, the small-ship luxury cruise line.

LAUREN HADLER

Head of international partnerships for the Kyotographie International Photography Festival, Lauren Hadler has been part of the festival's management team since its inception in 2013 and was previously director of education and public programs and director of exhibitions. She also works in production and sponsorship relations for the Kyotophonie Borderless Music Festival. She has diverse experience in the public and private sectors, working in interior and product design, exhibition, sponsorship, and marketing.

CRAIG MOD

Writer and photographer, Craig Mod emigrated to Japan as a teenager in 2000. His essays and photographs have appeared in *The New York Times, Eater, The Atlantic, The New Yorker, WIRED Magazine*, and others. He is the author of the books *Things Become Other Things* (2023), *Kissa by Kissa* (2020), *Koya Bound* (2016), and *Art Space Tokyo* (2010). He has never eaten at noma, but looks forward to the day he does.

JOJI SAKURAI

Asia-Pacific editor at the *New York Times* T Brand Studio, Joji Sakurai is also a freelance journalist and has written features for the *New York Times, Financial Times, Foreign Policy* and others. He has more than a decade of experience as the London-based enterprise editor for The Associated Press. Most of his formative education has been spent in izakayas, bistros, trattorias, pubs and other places of respectable repute.

SHUI ISHIZAKA

Born in Melbourne, Australia, and raised in Sydney, Shui Ishizaka made his way to Japan in 2018 to join Thomas Frebel in opening Restaurant Inua. After Inua's premature closure during the pandemic in 2020, Shui joined Sea Vegetable Company to build and operate a test kitchen researching new culinary applications for Japanese seaweed. In 2022, he joined the test kitchen team to develop the menu for Noma Kyoto.

AYA OKAMURA

An entrepreneur and cultural facilitator, Aya Okamura is a Japanese national who was born and raised in Copenhagen and specializes in bridging Danish and Japanese culture. The founder of Ayanomimi provides knowledge about culture, creative processes, and the Japanese business mindset, especially in the areas of lifestyle, design, and innovation. She also runs Olive Concept, a small-scale furniture producer. She coached the noma team in Japanese culture before they departed for Kyoto.

ROBERT YELLIN

For 26 years, starting in 1984, Robert Yellin lived in Shizuoka prefecture near Mount Fuji and established a gallery in the small city of Mishima. In 2011 he moved to Kyoto and his Yakimono Gallery of specialist pottery is in front of the Philosophers Path.

Nishiki Market

The journey to publish this magazine began more than fifteen years ago.

INTRODUCTION

RENÉ REDZEPI AND GABE ULLA

I CAN pinpoint the precise moment. It was in the days when serving a half-empty dining room was the norm for noma. I had walked into the office to meet with my wife Nadine who used to oversee the reservations. We performed our regular morning review of the books and one name stopped me in my tracks.

A two top under the name of Murata. Could it actually be him? The chef of Kyoto's Kikunoi, whose book on kaiseki cuisine I had just recently acquired? There was no way to tell. But just in case, I told the team to be ready to shift gears the second this mysterious party arrived. I asked the kitchen to prepare our extended menu, which back then was only offered at dinner. Then we waited.

The Murata I had hoped would materialize walked through our doors at 12:45, sharp. The sense of validation that rushed through me at the sight of him was instantly replaced by a very different emotion: Uh oh. Now we had to cook for him. The man graciously sat for the longest lunch we had probably ever served to anybody at that point. We were so eager. We were so young.

I waited until dessert to sheepishly greet the table. If Murata had been disappointed by the experience, he did a fine job of hiding it.

"I would love for you to visit us in Kyoto," he said.

A towering figure like Murata must tell people that all the time, I thought to myself. I didn't get my hopes up.

Less than six months later I was on a Finnair flight bound for Osaka. I made my way to Kyoto, where I spent two weeks under Murata's wing. I interned in the kitchen of the chef's hallowed Michelin three-star. I got to visit the city's best restaurants. I ate bear shabu-shabu in the mountains. I was also introduced to a concept that was starting to enter the culinary conversation in the west. Umami.

I left Kyoto smitten; I returned to Denmark energized. In a matter of months, we would come to understand so many of our region's ingredients in a new, much more complete way. We would double down on our nascent fermentation program, marking a major step in the development of what would become a hallmark of noma's cuisine. Somewhere along that path, more giants like Murata, from all over the world, started finding their way to our restaurant. Suddenly we were packed.

Yet almost every day I was visited by the same pang of yearning: I needed to go back to Kyoto—soon, and not just for vacation. Eventually, we arrived at the admittedly absurd idea—existing somewhere between a Herzog production and summer camp—of moving the entire noma team there to open a restaurant for three months. I don't mean a pop-up in the conventional sense; a real restaurant, one requiring the contributions of designers and architects, and a network of purveyors exactly like the one we rely on in Copenhagen. The only difference is that we would have weeks, not years, to pull it off.

One trusted fixer provided candid feedback: "You are

One week before opening.

Plating of the hassun serving.

out of your goddamn minds if you attempt this in Kyoto. It might work in the capital, where the noma name will mean something to some locals. Maybe." But Tokyo was hardly a tragic compromise, and far from a disappointment. Staging our first-ever international pop-up was a daunting challenge, but the whole undertaking proved strangely restorative. Back home, in the face of crushing demand, it wouldn't be unfair to say that creativity had to some extent taken a backseat.

The events that unfolded in the spring of 2020 made me long for the privilege of having a grind to complain about. Forget the end of noma. Was this the end of… everything? I had plenty of time to agonize over this and many more doubts during lockdown. To keep the dread at bay, I made a number of promises to myself, with Nadine as my witness. If we ever come out of this in one piece, we're doing another pop-up, was one of them.

The algorithm must have been listening. Thumbing through Instagram later that week, I stumbled upon photos of the new Ace Hotel in Kyoto, which had had its grand opening just before the pandemic. Designed by the illustrious architect Kengo Kuma, the property was as stunning as the timing of its launch was unfortunate. Right away I sent my colleagues the post and asked if they could reach out to the hotel. What did we have to lose?

To say that the Ace sprang into action would be an understatement. The project encountered a few frustrating setbacks, as you might expect during a global health crisis, but it happened. The first order of business on the ground fell to a dedicated research team, who explored the astonishing range of ingredients that would be in season by the time we opened: wild kiwis from Nagano, soybeans from Kansai. We enlisted artisans to craft plates and flatware. We hammered down the logistics. Everywhere we turned, everyone was so ready, so adaptable.

Nadine, our daughters and I touched down in Kyoto in January 2023. So did the members of the test kitchen. It was the dead of winter, the city was completely empty, and we were finally back to work. Worlds away from our usual routine, the creativity flowed effortlessly. It probably helped that we were drowning in quality: even in the colder months, Japanese ingredients will take your breath away.

From the beginning, we knew that Noma Kyoto was never going to bill itself as a kaiseki, or even Japanese, restaurant. That would be ludicrous. The idea was to be walloped by inspiration and tradition, and then fuse those learnings with our approach to create something new, something different. Not just for us, but for the locals as well. As the menu began to take shape, the vision was at last made real, not to mention delicious. The best work we've ever done.

The sous chefs have arrived.

Annegret and Mees going over the table plan.

And, just as they do back home, they spent their breaks at the restaurant trading notes. While I was in earshot of one such discussion, the realization hit me: without planning it, we had unleashed 103 extraordinarily curious individuals on one mythical city.

Soon the whole team was together in Japan, along with their spouses, significant others and children. Kindergarten, daycare, the daily commute route? It was all carefully arranged in advance and ready upon arrival, so everyone could hit the town without delay.

In the coming weeks and months, our team visited dozens upon dozens of cultural sights and even more restaurants. They played with monkeys in the countryside and planned daytrips to Naoshima and Lake Biwa. And, just as they do back home, they spent their breaks at the restaurant trading notes. While I was in earshot of one such discussion, the realization hit me: without planning it, we had unleashed 103 extraordinarily curious individuals on one mythical city.

The results of their adventures are the beating heart of this magazine, which takes special care to share information that would probably be difficult to access if you are not a local or a Japanese speaker. At minimum, these pages will help you find deliciousness when you go. That's for sure. But the greater hope is that they will inspire a few readers who are new to the subject to build a sustained relationship with Japan, whatever those words might mean to them, and see what happens. It's the best tip I could possibly give you.

On behalf of everyone at noma, thank you to the people of Kyoto for their trust, and for giving us the opportunity to do what we love when we really needed it.

A location blessed by nature, a thousand years of imperial history, auspicious feng shui, and religion have all contributed to Kyoto's unique cuisine and reputation as an eating destination.

CAPITAL DINING

KYOTO is like no other city. For more than 1,000 years it was the capital, the seat of the Japanese emperors and the focal point of the nation's religious and cultural life. And to this day it remains a repository of art, architecture, craftsmanship and intricate social structures developed over countless generations.

Everything promised by the tourist brochures is there: World Heritage Site temples with austere gardens of carefully raked gravel; parks that explode with cherry blossom in spring and scarlet maple leaves in fall; centuries-old ryokan inns and Noh theater stages, exclusive kaiseki restaurants and tea ceremony schools; low-rise neighborhoods of timber machiya houses.

Kyoto was the only major Japanese city spared destruction in World War Two, but over the past half century it has seen considerable redevelopment. It is now a large, modern city with a population of almost 1.5 million, bustling with all the usual trappings of 21st-century life: department stores, office buildings, sprawling suburbs, traffic jams, crowded subways, fast-food chains and convenience stores.

This tension between the echoes of the past and the buzz of contemporary life is what gives Kyoto its special, beguiling character. It may have become easier to live in, less proudly inward-looking, but it still keeps alive rituals and customs from every stage of its long history. The more you visit and return, the more of those layers you are likely to uncover, especially when it comes to kyo-ryori, Kyoto's distinctive cuisine.

Look at a map of central Kyoto and the first thing you notice is that it's laid out in precise alignment with the compass points, quite unlike the chaotic, haphazard neighborhoods of Tokyo. This is not a modern feature: it dates all the way back to when the city was founded in the year 794.

Surrounded by mountains on three sides and with the

Draped in history, Kyoto is the spiritual and cultural heart of Japan.

Kamo River flowing north-south down the middle, the location was considered especially propitious. Onto this site was superimposed a rectangular grid pattern that followed the same geomantic principles used in China's then capital, Chang'an (modern-day Xi'an).

The city was initially called Heian-kyo (Capital of Peace and Tranquility) but it has seen its share of warfare and destruction during its long history. Even so, the original template has always been rebuilt, with the emperor's palace at the apex and main thoroughfares running south, crisscrossed by streets numbered from one to nine. Fast forward some 1,200 years and that same layout is still helping residents and visitors alike to find their way around.

In 1868, following the overthrow of the shogunate that had held political power in Japan for the previous 265 years, the Emperor and his household relocated to Tokyo. However, the old imperial palace remained. And so did the artists, weavers, carpenters, calligraphers, priests, tea masters, wagashi confectioners and all the artisans whose skills and expertise underpinned the traditional rhythms of the capital.

With the palace empty, Kyoto no longer has a single focal point. But when it comes to eating, one key site is Nishiki-koji. Dating back to the city's earliest days, this narrow market street has played such a key role in feeding the city that it was given the nickname kyo no daidokoro: Kyoto's kitchen.

TODAY, NISHIKI MARKET is a magnet for visiting foodies, who browse and nibble at the numerous food vendors, eateries, producers and kitchenware dealers. Even so, many of the items on sale there would already have been familiar to Kyoto locals 1,000 years ago.

Tofu, dried seafood, kombu kelp, a multitude of pickles … these foodstuffs would all have been part of the formal banquets of the Heian aristocrats. Known as yūsoku-ryōri, this court cuisine from yesteryear can still be eaten at ryotei (high-end restaurants) in the city, such as two-Michelin-starred Mankamerou.

Kyoto's cuisine was limited by its landlocked location. The nearest fishing ports were 75 kilometers away, a one-day hike overland from the coast of Obama Bay (present-day Fukui prefecture). Before the advent of motorized transportation and refrigeration, it was impossible for fresh seafood to reach the capital without spoiling, so it had to be dried, salted or pickled.

Such was the demand for preserved seafood that the network of roads and mountain trails to Kyoto were dubbed the Saba Kaido, the mackerel highway. Carried on foot by peddlers, the fish would be used to prepare saba-bozushi, pressed onto long, rounded blocks of vinegared sushi rice. Today, one of the best restaurants still specializing in this sushi is Izuu.

Religion was another defining influence. From the city's

> By the time of the renowned 16th-century tea master Sen no Rikyu, tea gatherings would also include a meal, so that guests would not have to drink their matcha whisked tea on an empty stomach. Known as cha-kaiseki, these highly structured meals would incorporate multiple dishes, each prepared and served according to a prescribed order using ingredients reflecting the season.

earliest days, imperial edicts were issued banning the consumption of meat, especially from four-legged creatures. In mountainous areas, the hunting of wild animals continued, especially fowl, boar and deer, and the meat of dolphins and whales was conveniently classified as fish. But the consumption of red meat remained taboo among the general population until the late 19th century.

The arrival of Zen Buddhism from China in the 12th century brought with it a codified style of vegetarian cuisine governing the way the monks and priests ate. Called shojin-ryori, literally "devotion cuisine", it not only banned animal food, alliums and other pungent vegetables, it introduced new principles for balancing the flavors, colors and cooking methods.

Shojin cooking also introduced many of the dishes now considered standards of Japanese cuisine, including gomadofu (sesame tofu), konnyaku jelly, hijiki seaweed and namafu (wheat gluten). Many temples continue to offer shojin meals, not just for devotees but the general public, among them Kanga-an and Tenryuji.

Thanks to the influence of the temples, soy-based protein sources such as tofu and yuba (soymilk skin) soon became mainstream. Now these are indelibly associated with Kyoto, thanks to the quality and softness of the water that filters down from the nearby mountains into aquifers under the city.

Some of the earliest restaurants in Japan began as simple stalls serving tea and snacks for passers-by. Two structures erected outside Yasaka Jinja on the eastern flank of the Gion entertainment district were famous for dengaku, slices of tofu pierced with fine bamboo skewers, then grilled and slathered with miso.

Stalls in the long, covered arcades of Nishiki Market; crossing the Kamo River; Zen and the art of making tea.

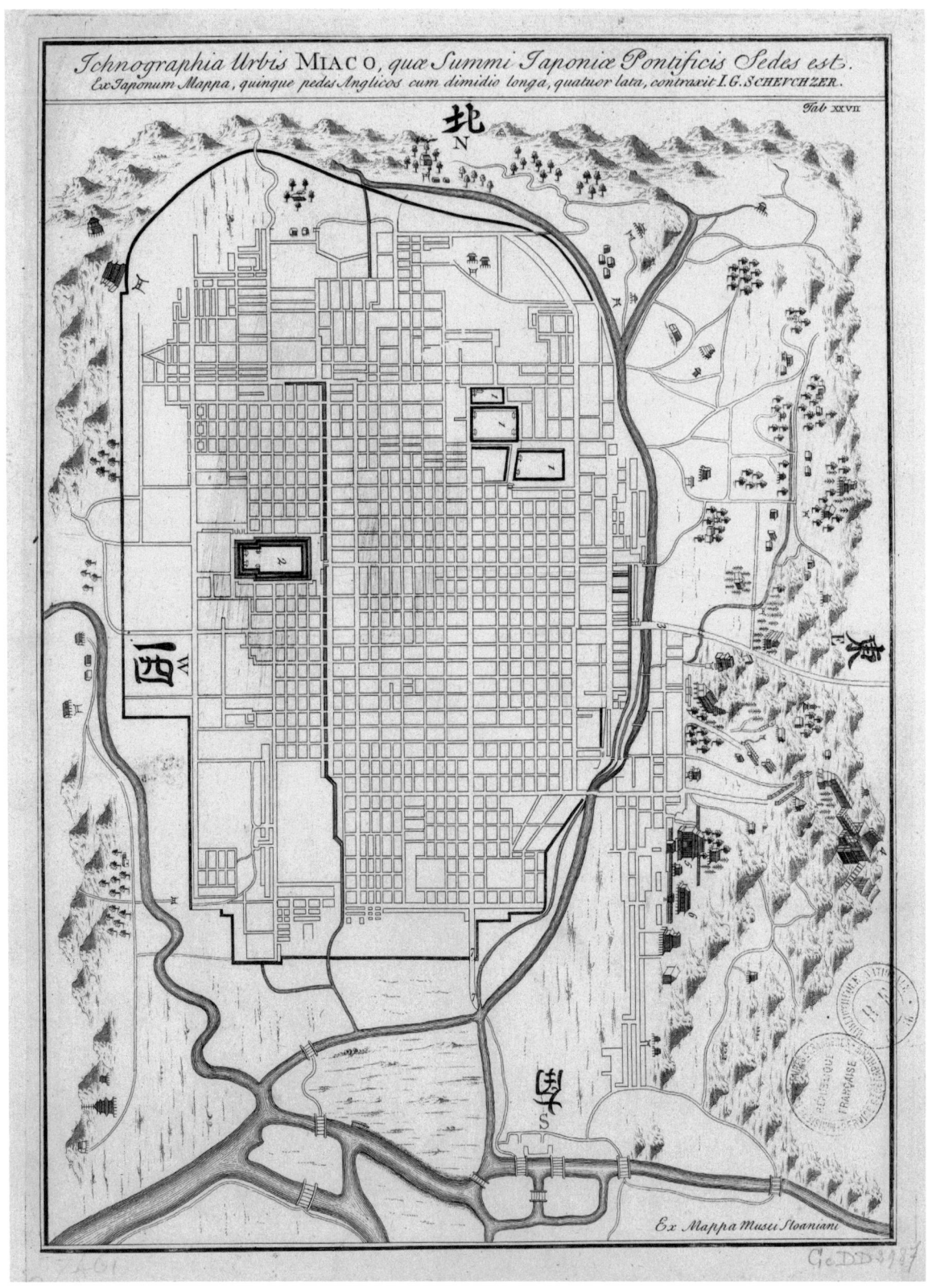

Kyoto was planned and built based on a grid pattern known as the Jō-Bō System borrowed from China, which originally divided the town into an eastern and a western part. The city was supplied by farmers who developed the region's unique vegetables.

Another popular dish was yudofu, hot-pots of tofu simmered in kombu dashi stock and served with a simple dip of shoyu (soy sauce) or ponzu (shoyu mixed with citrus or vinegar). Yudofu is said to have originated in the shojin-ryori served at Nanzen-ji temple in eastern Kyoto. That tradition lives on at specialist restaurants ranging from simple and rustic to elegant purveyors such as Yudofu Sagano, in Arashiyama, or Tousuiro.

There is much more to Kyoto than the busy central area defined by that central grid of congested streets. A short ride away to the northeast by suburban bus or train lies the tranquil, rural Ohara district. Famous for its beautiful Buddhist temple, Sanzen-in, the village is also renowned as a significant source of the produce that feeds the city's growing population.

Over the centuries, the local farmers developed vegetables unique to the region, often as offerings in the imperial court or for the annual rituals held at temples. There are now 31 traditional varieties that have been officially recognized as kyo-yasai (Kyoto vegetables).

Among the best known are the large, spherical shogoin turnips, which are mostly sliced and pickled; plump, purple kamo-nasu eggplants; delicate mizuna and mibuna greens; kujo-negi, a long green onion originally cultivated in the south of the city; and ebi-imo, a bulky corm that derives its name (literally, "shrimp taro") from its curved shape and horizontal stripes.

> But that is not the end of the story of Kyoto cuisine. In the last half of the 20th century, the kaiseki ethos sparked the imagination of many visitors from the West, making an impact on modern haute cuisine.

There is even a Kyoto brand of bamboo shoot (kyo-takenoko) that is cultivated in dedicated patches rather than foraged from the hillsides. Like most of these heirloom vegetables, it boasts a delicate texture and sweeter flavor than the wild varieties.

There is one other crop that has had a massive impact on life in Kyoto, molding the development not just of Japanese cuisine but also penetrating deep into the fabric of Japanese culture: *Camellia sinensis*, the plant known to the world as tea (cha).

Tea was reportedly first introduced from China in the late 8th century and initially its use was mostly confined to monasteries, where it was considered a medicine or meditation aid. But from the 12th century onward, the powdered leaves began to be used ceremonially.

By the time of the renowned 16th-century tea master Sen no Rikyu, tea gatherings would also include a meal, so that guests would not have to drink their matcha whisked tea on an empty stomach. Known as cha-kaiseki, these highly structured meals would incorporate multiple dishes, each prepared and served according to a prescribed order using ingredients reflecting the season.

Drawing on principles of shojin ryori, as well as the tea ceremony etiquette of omotenashi (mindful hospitality), this became the direct antecedent of the modern-day, multi-course kaiseki cuisine now offered at high-end restaurants in Kyoto and throughout Japan.

But that is not the end of the story of Kyoto cuisine. In the last half of the 20th century, the kaiseki ethos sparked the imagination of many visitors from the West, making an impact on modern haute cuisine. At the same time, chefs such as Yoshihiro Murata, the scion of the revered Kyoto kaiseki restaurant Kikunoi, traveled to France to study French cuisine. He has also been instrumental in helping many chefs to study and work in the city.

This two-way learning process continues, most notably in Noma Kyoto. Melding traditional Japanese ingredients and cooking methods with the inimitable approaches of the new Nordic cuisine represented another chapter of collaboration, innovation and evolution.

Liquid Life

Essential for life, water is the very compound on which Kyoto rests, a city favored by an abundance of pure, cool groundwater that has shaped the cuisine and sustained culture.

IN THE HEART of Kyoto stands Nishiki Market, arguably the city's most famous marketplace. Affectionately known as "the kitchen of Kyoto", it spans more than one hundred stalls, each with its own specialty ranging from fresh fruit and vegetables, seafood, meat, pickles and preserves, to sweets and confectionaries, tableware, kitchen tools and local street food. Although there is no official record of its beginnings, it is speculated that the market site has been a trading location for over a thousand years, long before being named Nishiki. The first record as an official marketplace dates from the 16th century when it was one the main hubs for wholesale fish and seafood.

Nishiki market's development and expansion, and how it directly correlates to the prosperity of Kyoto, stems from a single natural commodity: water. The site has long been blessed with cold, year-round, high-quality groundwater. During periods when ice was extremely precious and a commodity reserved only for nobility, an endless source of cold groundwater welling up in the Nishiki area meant seafood, meat and poultry wholesalers had the luxury of water that kept their products fresher for longer. Local fruit and vegetable purveyors also swear by preparing their preserves and pickles using this water.

The source of the water is 35 metres below the surface of Kyoto, a phenomenally sized basin roughly 33 kilometres long and 12 kilometres wide that holds more than 21 billion tonnes of water at any time, comparable to the volume of Japan's largest lake, Lake Biwa, which holds roughly 27 tonnes of water. Well access to this water isn't confined to Nishiki, and there are numerous wells throughout the city with great historic importance. Producers of Kyoto's greatest sake, tea, miso, soy milk and dashi have a trusted source of natural water that has served local artisans for generations.

But water sources aren't limited to the Kyoto basin, as many famous rivers both natural and man-made run in and out of the city. Kiyomizu. Izumikawa. Kawabata. Shirakawa. Izumi. Shimizu. Horikawa. Ogawa. Kawaramachi. Imadegawa. Miike. Oike. The entire city has a deep-rooted elemental affinity with water, and a large number of locations and landmarks are named for some form of association to water. Riverbanks, bridges and canals became central hubs for recreation and trade, playing a significant role in transportation, industry development and sustaining the general livelihood of the people. In some ways, the land Kyoto was built on was destined to bestow opulence; the abundance of water and ease of its access provided a unique cultural foundation befitting of Kyoto's thousand-year reign as the capital of Japan.

Japan is made up of four main islands surrounded by sea and ocean, however there are more than 10,000 islands that contribute to the Japanese archipelago. Because of the narrow form of this island nation, no point is more than 150 kilometres from a coastline. This unique yet understated geographical feature made one of the biggest impacts on Japanese culture as it developed. For everything from trade to transportation, resources to recreation, the proximity to the sea became an valuable asset in every region of the country.

Relentlessly curious, the Japanese people uncovered countless culinary delights, both animal and plant, from the sea. Learning how best to prepare these discoveries eventually led to technological advancements that facilitated supply and distribution. One might call it an endless search for food not necessarily for survival, but for deliciousness. The Japanese palate, always advanced, remains most in tune to the flavours of the sea; a race of people dedicated to delivering the innate quality of life that water gives, and expressing its purity on a plate.

Water has buoyed the fortunes of Kyoto through history.

Consideration of the guest is the soul of omotenashi. From a pine needle on a coaster to a tiny trinket evoking childhood memories, it is a belief system that goes way beyond hospitality.

OMOTENASHI

WRITING ABOUT Japanese omotenashi is a difficult task because it is such a profound concept compared to how hospitality is perceived in other parts of the world. It is an integral part of Japanese life, a way of living, and it is everywhere from convenience stores to the finest hotels and restaurants.

There are many diverse ways of hospitality and it varies from culture to culture. Within the food and beverage industry in Europe or America, many consider anything beyond basic service as hospitality—an elaborate bread basket, cheese or dessert trolley, water or wine glasses always filled, well-groomed and immaculately dressed servers who greet you with a smile. It is basically knowing what diners need and anticipating it; if performed before asked and better than expected, hospitality is achieved.

In China, hospitality shares some similarity with the west, but privacy is included. Knowing when to be present and when to disappear for the guests' secluded peace in a private room, tailor-made menus for regulars, making guests feel special, are core practices in Chinese hospitality.

But Japanese omotenashi is different and dissecting the word gives a good idea of the meaning. O is an honorific prefix, to address customers with respect. *Motenashi* means that there is no distinction between a surface action and the thought or motive behind it. In other words, it is the same inside and out. It is not superficiality.

After living in Japan for a few years, I've realized that omotenashi isn't just simple hospitality. In a Japanese restaurant, every second during the meal and beyond involves developing a personal relationship, partly through the food, partly through the interaction with the guest. Sometimes omotenashi is not even tangible or visible, it is a kind of feeling transferred through genuine sincerity.

The first time I felt omotenashi above and beyond western hospitality was at Ishikawa, a three-Michelin star kaiseki in Tokyo. It was raining and when I finished, Chef Ishikawa was already at the exit with his staff holding an umbrella for me. He walked me out for a bit and gave me the umbrella to take home. I had little kaiseki experience at that time, and thought it was such an incredible act. It still is, but I learnt that this is a form of omotenashi that almost every restaurant, even a very small eatery, will do for their customers.

Omotenashi can be extended to things that seem trivial or even nonexistent in our eyes, but not for the Japanese. When I was dining at Ogata, a kaiseki institution in Kyoto,

I asked for iced water. When I picked up the elegant glass, I saw a thin sliver of a pine needle on the antique-looking etched glass and silver coaster. I looked around and found that it was only present for my cold drink. I asked Ogata-san, about the lone pine needle on my coaster. He said: "This is because when ice melts, the glass turns wet and may stick to the coaster. The pine needle prevents that, so it's more convenient for you to pick it up."

Ogata-san said no one ever asked about it. It was a very small gesture indeed, and the pine needle was so fine it could easily have evaded attention. This happened in 2016 and I still remember this conversation vividly. Whenever I am in other restaurants and the coaster sticks to my glass (or worse, if it falls on my lap), I recall Ogata-san and this sublime Japanese omotenashi moment.

Kataori-san is the head chef of my favorite kaiseki restaurant Kataori in Kanazawa. I started going when they just opened, and Kataori-san and I became good friends. One time I posted online about my childhood collection of a Sanrio character Minna-no-Tabō, which filled all the bookshelves in my bedroom. When I visited him afterwards, he gave me a tiny little spoon with Minna-no-Tabō character printed on it. I was shocked. He said with a smile: "It is not easy to find." I had tears in my eyes. He told me to eat the owan (soup course) with it, then said: "Please give it back to me, I'll wash it for you and wrap it so you can take it home." My heart was filled with warmth. And before my birthday the same year, he gave me the teacup with the same pattern as a birthday gift to complete the set.

While omotenashi is a phenomenon that is practiced all over Japan, somehow it always feels that Kyoto manifests omotenashi to its fullest extent, perhaps because it is most comprehensible in kaiseki cuisine, the soul of Kyoto. It is also the city where ancient traditions of Japan, the kind of formality and tranquility with no pretentiousness are so well preserved.

For chefs who practice kaiseki cuisine, omotenashi is similar to the philosophy of cooking, where passion is applied wholeheartedly, daily trying to improve details to make it perfect. During cooking, they examine the execution of every micro-step to make it better. While practicing omotenashi, they look at every human touchpoint when serving a guest and try to make it perfect for the person. There is no end to the process of having enough omotenashi, there are an infinite number of things that could be considered depending on the relationship between the person and the situation.

The pursuit of excellence in omotenashi is an endless journey for the Japanese, and as a food lover I recognize the effort, passion and compassion invested by chefs and restaurants every day. I don't like to over-glamourize Japan and claim they do the best in everything. But when it comes to hospitality, it is indeed at another level, because omotenashi is practiced on a spiritual level, from the heart and soul.

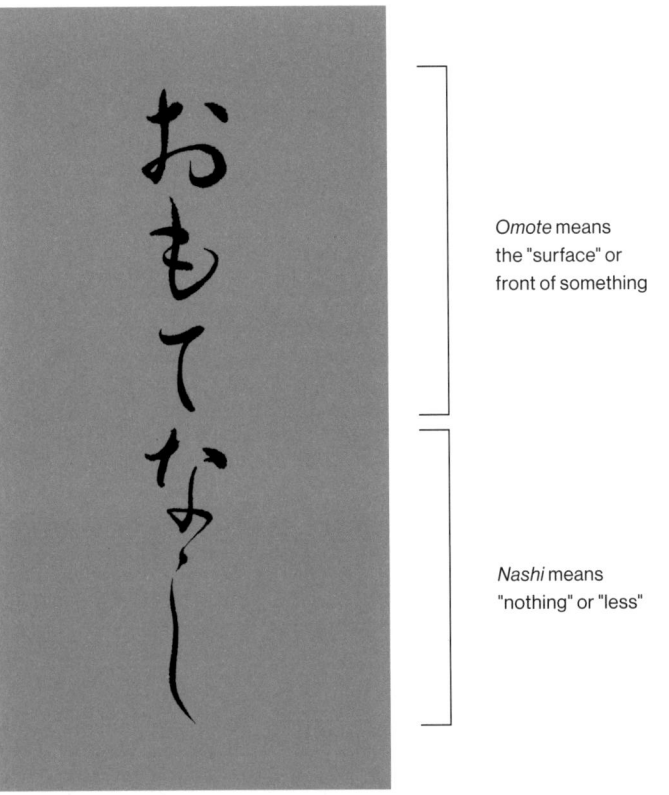

"Omote" means the front and implies that there is no back, which means that how you present yourself is how you are. You are not two-faced and you do not change how you act from person to person. "Nashi" means nothing, and based on its placement in the word, it denies the meaning of "omote", and implies that you have neither front nor back; you are simply acting genuine. This emphasizes that your heart motivates your actions. Nothing is done for personal gain and, conversely, you will do something even when it's not expected of you, just from the "goodness of your heart".

Omote means the "surface" or front of something

Nashi means "nothing" or "less"

Hospitality extends to the very last moment the guest is in sight.

Yoshihiro Murata understands tradition. He is the third-generation head chef of Kikunoi and for centuries his family were guardians of a special water source. But, as he tells René Redzepi, tradition can be a continuous, evolving element, provided it is powered by creativity, joy and deliciousness.

Q & A

RENÉ REDZEPI &
YOSHIHIRO MURATA

MASTER OF IMAGINATION

YOSHIHIRO MURATA was born in Kyoto, Japan, where his family has owned and operated restaurant Kikunoi since 1912. The restaurant was started by Murata-san's grandfather and after Yoshihiro's culinary training in both Japan and France, he returned to Kyoto in 1976 to work in the family business. Murata-san took over as the head chef of the original Kikunoi in 1993 and has been in charge ever since. Kikunoi is world-renowned and epitomizes kaiseki cuisine at its highest level.

In 2013, Murata-san was a crucial figure in promoting washoku, traditional Japanese cuisine to be recognized by UNESCO as an intangible cultural heritage. Murata-san is 72 years old and continues to manage Kikunoi daily.

RR: Konbanwa, Murata-san, and it is wonderful to see you. We would love to share the history of you, your family, and Kikunoi with our readers to give a bit of background to everything that you do. Murata-san, could you please share something about your family's history and your culinary heritage?

YM: In the beginning of our family history, we served the Toyotomi family at the Kodai-ji Temple. Our family were essentially Tea Monks, or chabozu, and we would travel with the shogunate to prepare tea for them. Kikunoi was the name of a fresh-water well that was used by the Toyotomi family—normal people were not allowed to use this water source until approximately 1860. Around 600 years ago, our family protected this water source which was used for tea ceremonies and their general needs.

Now aged 72, Yoshiro Murata took over as head chef of Kikunoi in 1993 and believes that doing something new every day has become a tradition, and the forward evolution of continuously creating new and fresh deliciousness has become the character of the restaurant.

> "To me, I am just freestyling. It's not about what tradition is or should be, but it's what I think tastes good. Some people talk about me as one of the persons who revolutionized cuisine. I'm not sure if it's true, but I still do cook what I want to eat."

When did you start operating as a restaurant?

Because our family worked for different samurai doing tea ceremonies, work disappeared for them around 1860 due to the Meiji Restoration period, when the country opened and the samurai disappeared. The Tokugawa government stopped providing subsidies which is why the work vanished—this occurred five or six generations before me. Our family was of course most focused on tea ceremonies, but we also served kaiseki food with the tea. After the Meiji Restoration, my family made the natural shift to focus on just food. My family's restaurant Kikunoi, started two generations before me in 1912.

Now that we're talking about your family's culinary heritage, could you speak about your father as a chef? Where did he train? And what were the values that he instilled in you?

My father and I are two different types of people. My father is very hardworking, traditional and focused. He is very by-the-book. I don't feel that I have the same personality as my father at all—he always took things very seriously and never faltered from this, so he and I are very different.

Then how did it go when you made the decision to continue the family tradition and get into cuisine?

Ironically, by going into cuisine, I was escaping from him. I aimed to be a French chef instead of a Japanese chef. I wanted to go to France to learn, so at the age of 21, I left Japan. Fifty years ago, when I made that move, nobody knew about Japanese cuisine in France—people didn't even know where Japan was on a map. When I was in Paris, I met a woman from the countryside and she had a photo of a samurai in her home. She asked me why I didn't have the same hair as a samurai. Back then, I realized that Japanese cuisine was culturally established in Japan, but so was French cuisine in Japan. I made the decision back then to make Japanese cuisine as well known internationally as French cuisine was. This became my life mission.

Was this goal something that you discovered while in France?

Yes, I made this realization while I was there. In Japan, I was taught that French, Japanese and Chinese were the three biggest cuisines in the world. However, when I went to France, I met many different people who had different points of view. I met Korean people who would say French, Chinese, and Korean were the most important cuisines. Thai people would say, French, Chinese, and Thai. This sentiment continued with everyone I met.

I remember being at the student canteen at university in France and some French students told me that they knew of Japanese cuisine as rice, soba, and they said "Japanese cuisine's nutrition is a complete disaster". These students were encouraging me to study French cuisine so that I could go back to Japan and contribute a French point of view on Japanese cuisine to improve it. This sentiment was quite provoking to me. At the time, I didn't quite understand why I got so offended by this attitude, but then it dawned on me, and I realized my deep love for Japanese cuisine. This innate pride of Japanese cuisine was why I got so upset with these students. That was why I left France and went back to Japan.

How long did you spend in France?

Eight months.

When you went back, was your father happy?

He was so mad that I left. Ironically, he was almost more mad that I came back, but this was his old Japanese way of thinking. He said, "You are a man and you made a decision to go to France but you come back after just eight months? What are you doing?"

But what happened when you came back? Did you begin to work with your father at Kikunoi? Did you begin to formulate a plan for the rest of your career and life?

When I came back, my father told me: "I supported your decision to go to France, and now that you're back, it's time you listen to me. So you must go to Nagoya to learn." So, I went to Nagoya to train at restaurant Kamome, a big restaurant on the top of a building. Inside it had many tables, a counter and a tatami room. I went to this restaurant to learn. I started at the bottom and worked there for three years and I tried to absorb as much as possible. It was hard work but it was a period in my life full of learning.

When did you come back to Kyoto from Nagoya? When did your father allow you to work with him in the family restaurant, and when did he allow you to impart your own ideas in Kikunoi?

When I came back to his place, he already had a lot of

> It's about sharing the fire of passion with others in life. If you can enlighten others, and therefore inspire others, you can get encouragement back again and be inspired by them. If they are inspired, I'm also inspired, and they can share their fire with me.

students and disciples. It was so difficult for me to be there. I did have some support from the head chef of Kikunoi, at the time—he was the chef just below my father in the hierarchy. The head chef would support me and give me encouragement. He treated me differently. The head chef would give me tasks to do in the kitchen, and then my dad would step in and send me outside of the restaurant to visit the bank or to fix stuff with the building. He knew I wanted to help, but he kept pushing me outside the kitchen. It was very difficult to just be there, so I began to consider the idea of starting my own restaurant. So, I asked my father to support me financially to start my own restaurant. And he said, "Why should I give you any money? I can loan you, but I won't give you it." And he loaned me 3 million yen which I had to pay back 50,000 yen every month. I was thinking, "50,000 is affordable", and so I started my restaurant, a branch of Kikunoi called Kikunoi Kiyamachi.

In the beginning it went okay, we had some guests, but eventually people stopped coming. There were many weeks with virtually zero guests. I sat down at the counter where the guests sit and started to read a lot of books: Japanese cuisine, Chinese cuisine, every kind of cuisine. Then I went to the grocery store, came back to the restaurant, and tried to cook something wondering if anyone would come to eat it. Some of the guests who went to my father's restaurant knew me from when I was young, and they would come and support me a few times a week. They asked, "What are you working with? What can you serve me?" And I served them, and they said, "This is not edible at all." They suggested, "What about cooking like this?" And they kind of consulted me. My father's friend and chef of another traditional restaurant in Kyoto called Tankuma came by my restaurant and drank beer, so I served some small dishes to him and then I asked him, "Don't you think this is a bit too sweet?", and he said, "Why are you serving me something and asking me something like that? Just give me something that is prepared properly that you are proud of." I said, "Well this is my father's recipe, and isn't this the proper way to serve food and respect my father?" He said, "What a stupid boy you are. If you think this is too sweet and you are not proud of it, why do you serve it? Cooking and serving a dish is about serving something that you think you would enjoy." This idea was a very important realization for me and has continued as an instruction for the next generation of Kikunoi. From that point on, I felt liberated and cooked what I wanted to cook. My father would say, "Don't serve any weird things that you do, this is not Japanese cuisine." So I said back to him that "I already decided to serve something that I want to eat, not strictly Japanese cuisine. I just want to do my absolute best." From that point on, my restaurant [Kikunoi Kiyamachi] began to get full.

To me, I am just freestyling. It's not about what tradition is or should be, but it's what I think tastes good. Some people talk about me as one of the persons who revolutionized cuisine. I'm not sure if it's true, but I still do cook what I want to eat.

You were only there for one year?

Kikunoi Kiyamachi was my branch of Kikunoi and I had this six-seat restaurant for three years. It is now known as Kikunoi Roan.

It's so interesting. To me, it's almost like you were using your restaurant as a test kitchen or a lab.

You're exactly right. It's where I found my freedom.

I would love to go back and see that period and taste your food back then. That would be such a joy. So in Japan—now that we're talking about tradition, and you were using your own place as a lab—how difficult is it to innovate when there's such a strong tradition?

To me, tradition is doing something new every day, and each day you draw a new dot. In the end, you can draw a line to connect those dots and this becomes tradition. Tradition is something that you create with your own hands; it's not just an old way of doing things which must be protected from progress. It's obviously different ingredients that we're using now compared to 100 years ago, and 100 years ago people were eating something else than what they eat now, so what they thought was delicious is not what people find delicious now. We cook with ingredients that exist right now for people who exist today. So, when you try to keep your guests happy, that means that you must evolve and continue forward, and this process of evolution itself becomes a tradition. At Kikunoi, we always try to do something new and fresh, and because of those efforts, that idea has become the character of Kikunoi.

I have to admit, when I eat at your restaurant, I can tell that you're experimenting. New spices, new flavors. It's always so interesting to eat.

If we can talk a little bit about creativity, I remember you spoke about having a "creative club."

Yes, this actually started in my father's generation. Chefs would gather, study, learn and try to serve something new. At that time, they revealed their own techniques, shared them with each other and then published their secrets. When we meet together now, we also share techniques, but really, we try to inspire each other.

Together? To each other?

Yes, serving dishes to each other, together. For example, now we're working on plant-based cuisine, and trying to make Japanese food without seaweed or katsuobushi.

How often do you meet?

Every month. We come with a dish and serve each other. Right now, we are nine people who bring dishes, and we criticize each other so strongly.

Do you think this is a uniquely Kyoto thing?

Yes, I think it's unique to Kyoto because all the chefs in Kyoto trust each other so much.

It's incredible and unusual to hear.

We criticize each other so much, and sometimes this could result in arguments if you don't trust each other, but we do. Trust is very important.

And people criticize you as well?

Yes, of course. So last time, I was asked, "Are you ill or unwell?" and I answered, "No, why?" They said, "Because nothing new happened to your dish!"

I find this so inspiring. As a foreigner, we look to Kyoto with its magnificent tradition, a historical place, alive with food, good restaurants in every corner of the city, and then to have the best chefs meet to push each other to be better and push tradition forward is very inspiring.

When we serve dishes at Kikunoi, we try to make them as if they were very traditional so that a 90-year-old woman won't recognize this is a new thing, but it is.

When speaking about Kyoto, you mentioned how people in France did not understand what Japanese cuisine was 50 years ago, but I still think people really don't understand it. How would you describe kaiseki?

I feel like the dishes you serve, or that French chefs serve, or the dishes that we serve, everything is actually kaiseki. The order of the dishes, the temperature, the timing of dishes—everything that you think through when you make

Murata is concerned about climate change and the future of the restaurant industry. He warns that the period of unlimited tasty and high-quality ingredients is almost over and urges chefs to work together.

a dish, and when you make a menu, you will ask the question: "At this point in the menu, guests will be pretty full, so what would they want to eat next?" To ask yourself such a question is in itself kaiseki. So, when I visited you at noma in Kyoto, I really felt like you made kaiseki. Tasting menus should be designed in a pattern where people feel very comfortable when they eat. The one who thought through this fact and became an expert was Sen no Rikyu [A Japanese tea master who mastered the art of the tea ceremony in the 16th century]. This was several hundred years ago, but today we still think about what is the most comfortable way for a guest to dine and still factor this into kaiseki. So, imagine that you make the first course, I make the second, you make the third dish, then a guest will be totally overwhelmed and happy: that is the spirit of kaiseki.

In kaiseki, is there an element of surprise? For example, Spanish cuisine focused heavily on the element of surprise for the last 20 years. Does that factor into kaiseki cooking?

Spanish cuisine, molecular gastronomy, that was one of the directions that food went at that time, but if you only focus on the avant-garde then it won't last. There is always something that will be new and change over time, but what do people always seek in the end? That will always be oishii—deliciousness. There should also be the element of having fun. But if you only think about this sort of stimulation and having fun, then you tend to lose track of deliciousness. I feel like what we seek within kaiseki is fantasy. What I want to create is something delicious for fantasy.

Imagination?

Exactly. Imagination. You dine with your mind, your heart, and your mouth.

Now we've spoken about how you started, the difficulties with your father, then you took over Kikunoi. I've met your son as he works in the kitchen now. How are you letting him find his way?

For me, it's about allowing him to do whatever he wants to [laughing]. You can't continue something that you don't feel is fun. I'm continuing to work every day at Kikunoi because I still genuinely enjoy it. You can never think about how many hours you have worked; the most important thing is that you can enjoy your work. I wish deeply that my son can find this sort of enjoyment in his own life so that he can create such a life himself. Having fun is the most important thing in life. I can't do anything if I don't feel joy—joy is essential.

How did you stay so motivated for over 50 years? Was it because of your purpose to spread Japanese cuisine throughout the world? Was that the primary motivation for you?

It's about sharing the fire of passion with others in life.

If you can enlighten others, and therefore inspire others, you can get encouragement back again and be inspired by them. If they are inspired, I'm also inspired, and they can share their fire with me.

Now that the fourth generation is in the kitchen of Kikunoi. Are you planning for 100 years from now? Or how do you plan?

I don't think about it as a plan, as such. I don't think that my son is thinking that deeply about the future either, but I am sure that all chefs will have a hard time in the future and that we do not have as many ingredients as we previously had. It's almost over that you can have unlimited ingredients that are tasty and high quality. What kind of steps forward do you take given this? Right now, I wish to have sea vegetable farms all over Japan. These farms can attract small fish, which will attract bigger fish, and in the next period of the world, I hope for everyone to eat and enjoy more sea vegetables in their daily diets. It's also fun to think like this, about the possibilities of the future. It's important to work for a more positive future.

Are you worried about the food of the future? Climate change, food scarcity?

Of course. On this day in July in Kyoto it is 38°C. All the vegetables dried up. More heat will come. How should we secure all the ingredients and food in general? What can we do about it at this moment? As a chef, you can't wait for politicians to take action. Chefs should, on a global scale, work together even more.

I totally agree with that. Cuisine moving forward has some uncertainties. Ingredients, climate change is one thing, but also a generational shift of young people not wanting to work in the industry.

But if you want to earn money, then you can't really stay in this industry. So, I just hope that we can gather with enough like-minded people, like me, that prioritize their life mission to create something better instead of amassing money. You don't really get to be wealthy in this industry. But we do have a unique industry. We get a guest that comes to dine, they pay, they say thank you, and then they will come back. There aren't many industries that give you access to such people. If you're a doctor, your customers are sick people. Lawyer's customers are people that have problems. In restaurants, our guests are generally pretty happy and healthy people. They enjoy a meal, say thank you, and then pay. That's not so bad.

If you had a message to all the future young cooks out there. What do you think they should be thinking about and caring about today?

Chefs need to work together to create a better world. This needs to be the motivation for the work that we do. If we do work together, I'm certain that we can create a better world in the future. When you have money you can drive a nicer car, have a bigger house, you have better clothing, but what else can you do? It's probably pretty limited with money. We need for future chefs to think the same and share the same values—to not just think about money, but to want to work for a better world.

Better world, more collaboration.

We need unity through chefs across the world.

It makes a lot of sense what you are saying. We love the advice. Here at the end, can I ask some questions about Kyoto? I assume that since you started cooking 50 years ago, the city has changed a lot. How do you feel that change? What has shifted?

A positive change is that people are rich enough to go out and eat. At the very least, people can go out to eat if you have an anniversary or some other special occasion. For people to have the means to share these moments is a very good thing.

And regarding tourism?

Well, we certainly get a lot more tourists now than we did 50 years ago. At Kikunoi, we must set limits. If we don't have any limit, our restaurant will be fully booked by foreigners, so we limit it to 40 percent foreigners so that we can still serve mostly local, Japanese people.

Wow. So, do you feel that the city of Kyoto (because I don't know it the way you do), is it a good moment for the city? Is it currently vibrant? Full of life and creativity?

Probably too good, to be honest [laughing]. Of course, the tourism is good for us, but there are other parts of Japan to visit [laughs again].

Thank you so much Murata-san for taking the time to speak with us.

Thank you so much. It would be wonderful for our sort of relationship to continue into the next generations.

I hope so too, thank you again Murata-san.

I'm continuing to work every day at Kikunoi because I still genuinely enjoy it. I can't do anything if I don't feel joy—joy is essential.

WORDS — SHUI ISHIZAKA, HEAD OF PROJECT RESEARCH

The juxtaposition of clutching the traditions of the past with one hand, the other hand outstretched to its limits reaching for every possibility that exists in the future: this is how I personify Japan.

A PERSON OF TWO CULTURES

ILLUSTRATION: PAULA TROXLER

BEING BORN and raised in Australia, words cannot express the gratitude I have for my mother and father who cooked meal after meal using every form of Japanese produce and condiments they had access to. As a child, terms such as umami and dashi, ingredients such as kombu or miso would be thrown around the kitchen at home, and they're the same buzz words being thrown around some of the world's best restaurants some 30 years on. Though many other facets of my upbringing are as Australian as they come, I have grown to channel what I know of my Japanese heritage and it reflects how I go about creativity. Living and cooking in Japan for five years now, I've never been more grateful for the way my perception of the world has developed; definitely not as a Japanese person, but not as a pure Westerner either.

It is truly fascinating to connect to the people and the places, and become more familiar with the intertwining threads that both preserve and create Japanese culture. Everything seems to exist in peaceful contradiction. There exists an organisation charged with preserving the woodwork of the oldest temple in Japan, an art that stopped being practiced in mainstream architecture centuries ago. In another part of the country, a group of creative minds is drawing up a blueprint for a building to be the hallmark of 21st-century architecture. One day someone might attend a kabuki theatre, a type of performing art that has existed since the 16th century, and on the same day elsewhere 10,000 people gather to see a Vocaloid virtual idol performing a concert completely synthesised through CGI. The juxtaposition of clutching the traditions of the past with one hand, the other hand outstretched to its limits reaching for every possibility that exists in the future: this is how I personify Japan.

The culinary world, however similar it is in many ways, I feel is much less daring. Teachings of traditional Japanese cuisine have been developed and passed down religiously with great discipline, its deliciousness only exceeded by its purity. For every dish representative of Japanese cuisine, there have been cooks throughout history and even now who've decided to devote their lives to honing every minute detail that the dish comprises. Take a humble bowl of rice. To us, all you need is rice, water, a pot, and a heat source. But to someone who's devoted their lives to cooking the perfect bowl of rice, it starts where the rice is grown and when it's harvested; how much the rice is polished, how it's washed and steeped; what kind of water and the design of the clay pot it's cooked in. I feel this school of thought is what lies at the very core of creativity in the Japanese kitchen. What can be subtly manipulated? How would we incorporate the human touch without masking or erasing the inherent qualities this ingredient holds? This is what creates the foundation of artisanal Japanese cookery. If this is an example of the proverbial hand keeping traditions of the past protected, what of the other hand, outstretched toward the future?

> There's no denying the existence of endless wisdom throughout the pages of history, but to create something truly new often requires an amount of understanding and respect for the past that can make a delicate balance between tradition and innovation.

Over the last five decades, there have been thousands of chefs that have travelled to food Meccas such as France and Italy to learn cuisine, bring it back to Japanese soil to practice what they've learnt and adapt it to Japanese ingredients. Godfathers of cuisine in these countries have also opened branches in Japan. However, very few chefs in Japan have chosen to completely reimagine what it means to collaborate with farmers, producers and craftsmen, and cook within Japan in the 21st century. Just because something has been done a certain way for the last 100 years, doesn't mean it has to for the next 100. There's no denying the existence of endless wisdom throughout the pages of history, but to create something truly new often requires an amount of understanding and respect for the past that can make a delicate balance between tradition and innovation. Being so intimately involved in the creation and execution of Noma Kyoto was without a doubt the closest I've been to witnessing this balance being achieved in Japan.

A group of curious minds, curious enough to want to know how everything has been done before, reproduce it, only to deconstruct it again to apply the very same curiosity to explore its unfound possibilities. It's a thought process that transcends the culinary world, one that I personally endeavour to apply to my own creativity both in and out of the kitchen.

Each spring, a pink wave of cherry blossom sweeps north over all of Japan, a visible example of the progression of microseasons and different microclimates that furnish an abundance of unique produce across the country.

CYCLE OF SEASONS

> When cherry blossoms bloom, they bloom in unison like a breathtaking display of fireworks. They will never wilt and whither on the tree, rather, they fall with the wind or rain. When they fall, they fall not as a flower, but as individual petals falling like snow in a gentle breeze.

THE TRADITIONAL Japanese calendar marks the passing of the seasons and changes in nature's temperament through names and phrases given to different moments of the year. There are 24 divisions called nijūshi-sekki and within each division, or sekki, are three fleeting moments that form shichijūni-kō. These are the 72 microseasons that form an annual journey through a year in Japan when the land awakens to life, thrives, then returns to a deep slumber. In the same way mankind created poetry as a form of human expression, each of these subtle seasonal cues that nature provides became a deep cultural base that guided the Japanese people on how to eat, feel, and celebrate throughout their lives.

Arguably nature's biggest seasonal cue in Japan is the blooming of cherry blossoms. Synonymous worldwide with the coming of spring in Japan, this particular microseason lasting four days from March 25 to 29 is called sakura hajimete hiraku, which literally translates to first cherry blossoms bloom. It's a spectacle for those who witness it for the first time just as it is for those who've seen it every year for their whole lives into old age. In the winter months, sakura trees all around the country ready an excessive number of flower buds on their branches. As the mornings get warmer, the whole country awaits in great anticipation for the day they wake up to see their neighborhood sakura trees burst in a pale pink flush.

There are numerous other spring flowers in Japan. Cherry blossoms are neither the first nor the last to appear, are not rare in the slightest and singularly not the most beautiful. So why renowned above all else? Some sources say the country's love originated from the Emperor's love for cherry blossom viewing during the Heian period. He would regularly sponsor cherry blossom viewing events for the people of the country, creating one of the very few cultures that both nobility and commoners could enjoy. As time passed, the delicate beauty and simplicity of cherry blossoms became a common motif in Japanese literature, oftentimes a symbol for life and death.

Cherry trees themselves are long-lived with some varieties surviving over 100 years, yet their flowers, despite their beauty, are extremely short-lived. When cherry blossoms bloom, they bloom in unison like a breathtaking display of fireworks. Under normal circumstances they will never wilt and whither on the tree, rather, they fall with the wind or rain. When they fall, they fall not as a flower, but as individual petals falling like snow in a gentle breeze.

Cherry blossoms were, and still are, a figurative expression of how to live one's life: make the most of "your time to shine", remain graceful to the minute you bow out, no matter how short and fleeting your time on this earth. It is a time for a moment for self-reflection on the year since one last witnessed the cherry blossoms' bloom.

Cherry blossom viewing is still widely practiced today. It can be as casual as walking your dog down the riverbank, a picnic under blooming branches, or an annual festival that brings the whole town to life. The joy that cherry blossoms bring to the nation developed a unique culture of a time to be together with friends and family, much like Christmas and Thanksgiving in the Western world. An annual occurrence as significant as this, without doubt is one of the most memorable seasons. The appearance of cherry blossoms, however, is not to be thought of as the first sign of spring.

According to the old lunar-solar calendar, the first season of the year is called risshun. The first day of risshun, comes the day after setsubun, a historic national festival held on the second or third day of February every year to signify the end of winter. Despite the stereotypical imagery associated with spring, February in Japan remains the coldest period of the year, a time of struggle to survive throughout history. Predecessors believed that perseverance through this trying period would always bring light and warmth, a sentiment of joy and anticipation that has engrained itself into the notion of risshun, with a little more sunlight and a little less snow as each day passes. It's a time of the coming of new life and preparations to welcome the lavish bounty of the season ahead.

Cherry blossoms and the first ingredients of spring delivered by farmers and foragers, spark excitement and emotion.

Kyoto vegetables and sansai from the mountains surrounding the ancient city.

ALTHOUGH its use is not entirely limited to spring, the word hatsu is a commonly overheard buzzword throughout restaurants and marketplaces during this time. It's a word meaning first, and ingredients delivered by farmers and foragers during this season tend to spark a unique sense of excitement and emotion amongst the people, with connotations of good fortune, good health, and most important of all, great flavour associated with the very first of its kind to come out of the ground that year. After many cold months of cooking with a range of seasonal root vegetables, game meat, ferments and preserves from the previous summer, restaurant chefs and home cooks alike have plenty to be excited about. The gentle warmth in the air orchestrates young leaves, shoots, and sprouts to grow, some even emerging from beneath the last layer of snow. This seasonal cue applies to the wide range of fruit and vegetable farmers across the country who carefully plan their crops and fields. However, nature also runs its own theatre of wild produce simply categorized as sansai.

Sansai literally translated means mountain vegetable, and it encapsulates hundreds of varieties of edible greens that burst to life all along the mountain tops and hillsides across the country throughout the spring season. Tender, delicious and extremely nutritious, historically sansai has been an indispensable source of food during times of economic hardship. People learnt to utilize what nature provided freely and in abundance, whether foraged to cook and consume fresh, or preserved to sustain the following winter. Many of the older generation today still take to their local mountainside every year seeking these wild treats. Restaurant chefs with the right know-how, often source the best of what they can find to serve on their menus, providing an eloquent and momentary reflection of time and place.

Despite Kyoto having plentiful local fresh produce, both farmed and wild, its history of being the capital of Japan for more than a thousand years means it had (and still has) great access to the best of what each province along the Japanese archipelago has to offer. The landscape and terrain, and the way the very country is shaped allows exploration of its bounty in a unique way. The change in weather and temperature can be observed as a metaphoric wave ascending the country then descending as the seasons come and go. If an ingredient's peak season is dictated by the climate of where and when it grows, Japan has the luxury of multiple peak seasons of its fruit and vegetable. Given the country's topography and elevation, two locations hundreds of kilometres apart may provide identical growing conditions albeit with a delay of a few weeks the further away from the equator it is. The week of late-season bamboo shoots in one location may very well be the same week of hatsu bamboo shoot elsewhere. Different sun, soil, and water means that two farms in the east and the west practicing the same farming method, producing the same variety of citrus may yield completely different expressions of the fruit. This kind of variation provides endless possibilities when it comes to creativity, as these differences are all it takes for certain types of produce to lend itself to particular applications.

To study and to know when key microseasons hit specific areas of the country is a lore that takes a lifetime to grasp, but just understanding the concept and having a close eye on weather forecasts can be an indispensable aid when it comes to obtaining what truly is the best the of its kind available at any given time.

> Sansai literally translated means mountain vegetable, and it encapsulates hundreds of varieties of edible greens that burst to life all along the mountain tops and hillsides across the country throughout the spring season.

72 MICROSEASONS

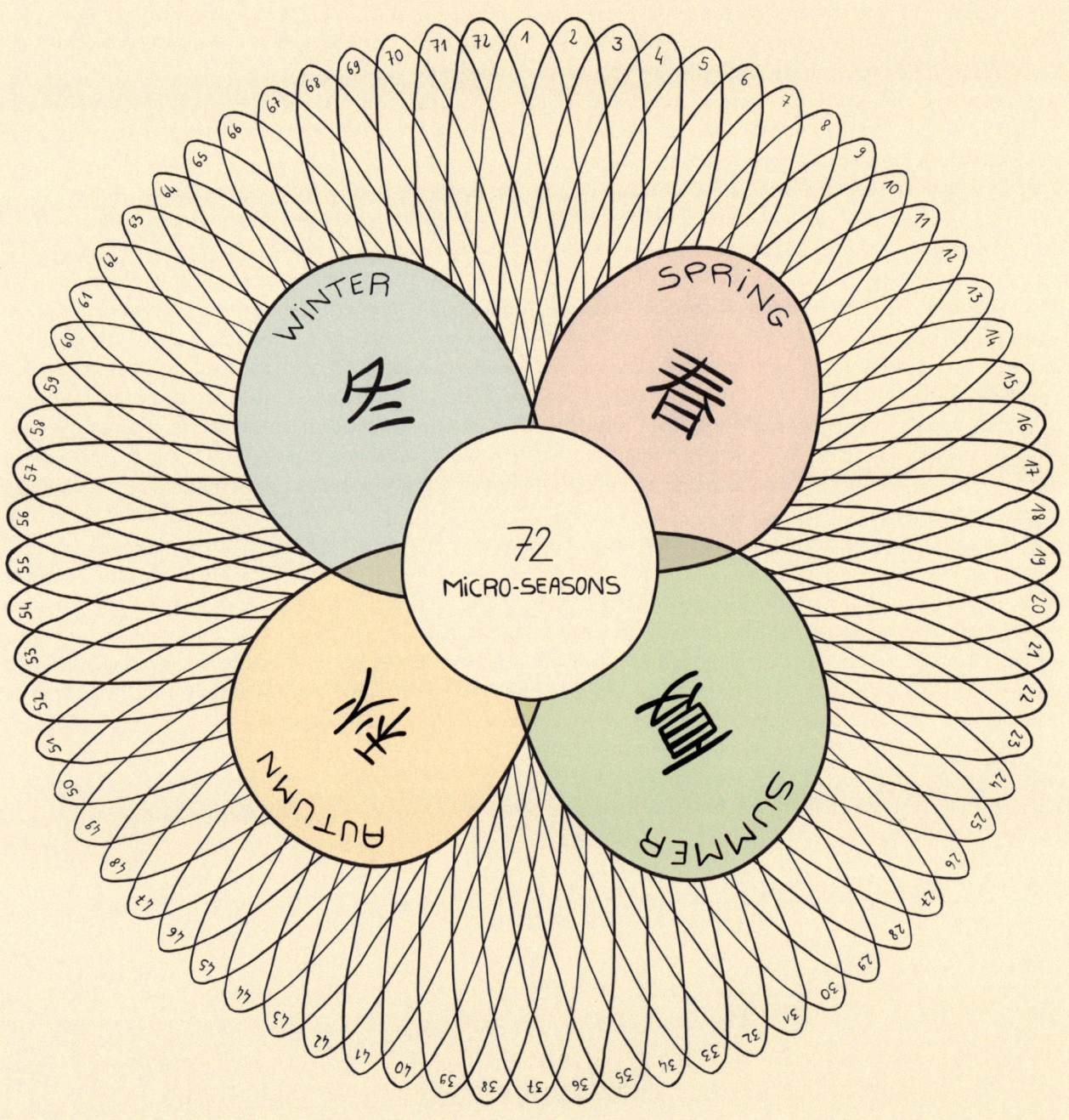

The wisdom of the ages segments the cycle of the season into lyrical divisions.

RISSHUN (立春)		**BEGINNING OF SPRING**		**RIKKA** (立夏)		**BEGINNING OF SUMMER**
1	Feb. 4–8	The east wind melts the thick ice.		19	May 5–9	Frogs begin croaking.
2	Feb. 9–13	Bush warblers sing in the countryside.		20	May 10–14	Worms wriggle to the surface.
3	Feb. 14–18	Ice cracks, allowing fish to emerge.		21	May 15–20	Bamboo shoots sprout.
USUI (雨水)		**Rain Water**		**SHŌMAN** (小満)		**Lesser Fullness**
4	Feb. 19–23	Rain falls, moistening the soil.		22	May 21–25	Silkworms feast on mulberry leaves.
5	Feb. 24–28	Mist lies over the land.		23	May 26–30	Safflowers bloom in abundance.
6	Mar. 1–5	Trees and plants put forth buds.		24	May 31–June 5	Barley ripens, ready to be harvested.
KEICHITSU (啓蟄)		**Insects Awakening**		**BŌSHU** (芒種)		**Grain in Ear**
7	Mar. 6–10	Hibernating insects emerge.		25	June 6–10	Praying mantises hatch and come forth.
8	Mar. 11–15	Peach trees begin to bloom.		26	June 11–15	Fireflies fly out from moist grass.
9	Mar. 16–20	Cabbage whites emerge from their cocoons.		27	June 16–20	Plums ripen, turning yellow.
SHUNBUN (春分)		**Spring Equinox**		**GESHI** (夏至)		**Summer Solstice**
10	Mar. 21–25	Sparrows begin building their nests.		28	June 21–26	Prunella flowers wither.
11	Mar. 26–30	Cherry blossoms begin to bloom.		29	June 27–July 1	Irises bloom.
12	Mar. 31–Apr. 4	Thunder rumbles far away.		30	July 2–6	Crowdipper sprouts.
SEIMEI (清明)		**Fresh Green**		**SHŌSHO** (小暑)		**Lesser Heat**
13	Apr. 5–9	Swallows return from the south.		31	July 7–11	Warm winds blow.
14	Apr. 10–14	Wild geese fly north.		32	July 12–16	Lotuses begin to bloom.
15	Apr. 15–19	Rainbows begin to appear.		33	July 17–22	Young hawks learn to fly.
KOKUU (穀雨)		**Grain Rain**		**TAISHO** (大暑)		**Greater Heat**
16	Apr. 20–24	Reeds begin to sprout.		34	July 23–28	Paulownia trees begin to produce seeds.
17	Apr. 25–29	Rice seedlings grow.		35	July 29–Aug. 2	The ground is damp, the air hot and humid.
18	Apr. 30–May 4	Peonies bloom.		36	Aug. 3–7	Heavy rains fall.

RISSHŪ (立秋)		**BEGINNING OF AUTUMN**		**RITTŌ** (立冬)		**BEGINNING OF WINTER**
37	Aug. 8–12	Cool winds blow.		55	Nov. 7–11	Sasanqua camellias begin to bloom.
38	Aug. 13–17	Evening cicadas begin to sing.		56	Nov. 12–16	The land begins to freeze.
39	Aug. 18–22	Thick fog blankets the land.		57	Nov. 17–21	Daffodils bloom.
SHOSHO (処暑)		**End of Heat**		**SHŌSETSU** (小雪)		**Light Snow**
40	Aug. 23–27	Cotton bolls open.		58	Nov. 22–26	Rainbows disappear.
41	Aug. 28–Sept. 1	The heat finally relents.		59	Nov. 27–Dec. 1	The north wind blows leaves off the trees.
42	Sept. 2–7	Rice ripens.		60	Dec. 2–6	Tachibana citrus trees begin to turn yellow.
HAKURO (白露)		**White Dew**		**TAISETSU** (大雪)		**Heavy Snow**
43	Sept. 8–12	White dew shimmers on the grass.		61	Dec. 7–11	The skies stay cold as winter arrives.
44	Sept. 13–17	Wagtails begin to sing.		62	Dec. 12–16	Bears hide away in their dens to hibernate.
45	Sept. 18–22	Swallows return to the south.		63	Dec. 17–21	Salmon swim upstream en masse.
SHŪBUN (秋分)		**Autumnal Equinox**		**TŌJI** (冬至)		**Winter Solstice**
46	Sept. 23–27	Thunder comes to an end.		64	Dec. 22–26	Prunella sprouts.
47	Sept. 28–Oct. 2	Insects close up their burrows.		65	Dec. 27–31	Deer shed their antlers.
48	Oct. 3–7	Fields are drained of water.		66	Jan. 1–4	Barley sprouts under the snow.
KANRO (寒露)		**Cold Dew**		**SHŌKAN** (小寒)		**(Lesser Cold)**
49	Oct. 8–12	Wild geese begin to fly back.		67	Jan. 5–9	Parsley thrives.
50	Oct. 13–17	Chrysanthemums bloom.		68	Jan. 10–14	Springs once frozen flow once more.
51	Oct. 18–22	Crickets chirp by the door.		69	Jan. 15–19	Cock pheasants begin to call.
SŌKŌ (霜降)		**First Frost**		**DAIKAN** (大寒)		**Greater Cold**
52	Oct. 23–27	Frost begins to form.		70	Jan. 20–24	Butterburs put forth buds.
53	Oct. 28–Nov. 1	Drizzling rain falls gently.		71	Jan. 25–29	Mountain streams gain a cover of thick ice.
54	Nov. 2–6	Maple leaves and ivy turn yellow.		72	Jan. 30–Feb. 3	Hens begin to lay eggs.

PHOTOGRAPHY DITTE ISAGER

THE STORY OF NOMA KYOTO IN TWENTY SERVINGS

The test kitchen team gives a taste of the creative process, imagination, collaboration and sheer fun that went into creating some of the dishes on the menu that drew from both Japan and noma. As told to Adam Sachs.

METTE BRINK SØBERG
Head of the test kitchen

JUNICHI TAKAHASHI
Head of the test kitchen

THOMAS FREBEL
Creative director

MIREK ANDERSON
R&D chef

DHRITI ARORA
R&D chef

SHUI ISHIZAKA
Head of project research

"Our heads were full of ideas," Mette Søberg, head of the test kitchen, says of their first research trip to Japan in 2020. *"This was a really impactful trip. We stayed in temples, did a lot of meditation and tried to just dive into this way of life. We're trying to build this creative machine and fuel ourselves. And then there was this this long period where we weren't really able to do things. And what we love about working at noma is that everything is possible. You think, "Ah, this is crazy. No way it's gonna happen", and then somehow we make it happen. So it felt like such a beautiful return. And I have to say, I think the creativity leading up to the pop-up in Japan was probably the most kind of free-flowing and spontaneous that I've experienced in my time at noma."*

SERVING NUMBERS ONE TO FIVE

Hassun

Five small bites, focused and intricate. Clockwise from 6 o'clock: yuba with grilled ramson, red ginger and koji, rose and tomato, black garlic and cherry leaf, tomato gel with pollen.

JUN: Hassun, traditionally, is the first serving in a Kaiseki meal and is defined by the flavors of the season through small bites on one plate. They are often represented by ingredients from both the Sea and the Mountains.

Hassun was originally served during religious ceremonies on plates that roughly measured 24 centimeters by 24 centimeters. The word Hassun can be broken into two parts: Ha(s) and Sun. Hachi is the Japanese word for the number 8, and in this instance, the chi sound is dropped from the word. Sun is an old Japanese measurement - 1 *sun* is 3.03cm. Thus, combining Ha(s) with Sun yields 8 times 3.03: the measurement of the plate used for Hassun servings in religious ceremonies.

Today, hassun is served in almost every style of Japanese restaurant that exists in Japan, but the way in which it is served can vary widely from restaurant to restaurant. We created our hassun serving with respect to the history of Japanese cuisine, but through our own interpretations and creativity.

MIREK: When we first got back to Japan and started the R&D, René [Redzepi] said at the first meeting he wanted to do a hassun. Sort of like a homage to kaiseki tradition which is such a part of Kyoto cuisine.

METTE: We always talk about how it's important that we have a very impactful beginning to the menu so that as soon as the guests arrive at the restaurant, they sit down and when they get the first dish, it's like, "Okay, wow." We always try to make first dishes that are very impactful. Flavor, of course, is always the most important thing for us. But I would say at the beginning of the menu, the feeling that you get when the first dish arrives at the table is very important. It needs to be something where people really feel the sense of where they are and what time of the year.

MIREK: Traditionally a hassun would have something from the ocean, something from fresh water, something wild and from the forest floor. It would taste very simple, of itself—but ours had high umami notes, high acid notes, high textural notes. Ours is like an uppercut hassun. Texture was very important. The cherry leaf for instance is salted and preserved in season. We washed the salt off, cooked it in a bag to soften it. Then we would brush a paste of black garlic on it and dry the black garlic onto the actual leaf. You get this salted cherry flavor. It's like a leather roll-up but nowhere near as chewy.

DHRITI: Sometimes when we work on a dish, unintended consequences occur, and the cherry leaf was one instance of this. We were working on different imprints of leaves on different fruit leathers in an attempt to fold them into origami—I even made a black garlic praying mantis [laughing]. After a lot of trial and error, we discovered that the enzymes present in the black garlic helped to break down the cell structure in the cherry leaf itself which resulted in a more tender bite.

METTE: One thing that's come from the pop-ups is we've become much better at understanding what works together. We're quite lucky at the moment that we have a group of people that looks at things quite differently. Jun, for example, loves to put a million different things together. Sometimes we refer to him as the umami tsunami! Because he's good at utilizing all these different ferments and all these different umami drops that we have. He's just really great at mixing 30 different ingredients together and then making it taste amazing.

JUN: When you work with small bites, they must have exceptional flavor. One bite, there has to be big impact. Some things we realized it's better not to make ourselves. Like yuba. We visited these people making such amazing products. They know how to make it perfect and have been doing it for so long, why not collaborate with them rather than try to recreate it in our small kitchen?

METTE: Of course it's a bit crazy from a kitchen perspective to actually put together five small dishes that are as elaborate as those dishes were. And we're working in a much smaller space than we're used to, but this has also been amazing for the kitchen, because now when we're back in Copenhagen, it's easy to see that we have it pretty good! I think this made for a really strong opening also for us as a team, and it was more fun because it meant that everyone had to be involved in the first serving.

SERVING NUMBER SIX
Seaweed Shabu Shabu

A boiling hotpot of smoked wakame stem and pine dashi with seasonal fresh seaweed and sea buckthorn ponzu.

THOMAS: Temperature is a constant conversation. When was the last time you were sitting in a fine dining restaurant and you had to wait for your food to cool down? There's a different satisfaction to eating something really, really hot. Slurping some noodles out of a hot ramen bowl is just incredible. That's why we felt like the hot pot serving was so important for the menu. Temperature is such an important part of making a menu. It's complicated and underestimated.

METTE: We wanted to pay respect to Japanese culture and cooking techniques—but also to have a bit of fun. Here you get this pot that was really hot with steam coming out. You take various seaweed with chopsticks and dip them into this bubbling broth. This reminded us a little of the kind of dish we had in the temple when we were exploring shōjin ryōri on an early research trip to Kyoto.

SHUI: We had to take baby steps, just to try certain things, to see how the seaweed would react to certain methods of cookery, and take it from there. Boiling it, grilling it, baking it—just see how each particular type of seaweed would react. Building a base knowledge of what we're working with, what it likes to be, how it likes to be prepared, how it doesn't like to be prepared.

METTE: It seems like a fairly simple dish, but the whole process is so much more complicated than it seems at first. Before the beautiful wakame roots are cooked in the broth, you have to cook them in koji oil and then hang them above the barbecue for two days, so they get the smoke. It's like why does it have to be so complicated? [laughs]

SHUI: I work on culinary R&D for a company called Sea Vegetable that farms seaweed in all the seas of Japan. In Japanese seas alone there are over 1,500 varieties of seaweed. Even in Japan, with such a deep culture of eating seaweed, they only eat 50 to 100 types, meaning there's 1,400 varieties that have still yet to make it on the plate, that are yet to have their potential unlocked. So to try this variety of seaweed, I think it was just as eye-opening for us as it was for our guests.

METTE: Normally when we taste a dish for the very first time, there's still a long way to go. But with this dish, Shui served it and it was pretty much ready to go.

SHUI: There were many different renditions and many, many different ways of preparing seaweed that came before we arrived at this particular dish. I guess it's like when you lose something it's in the last place you look. Seaweed shabu-shabu was the dish that came last. It almost made too much sense.

SHUI: The vast majority of the guests are well versed in culinary delights. But I doubt they have had a vegan shabu-shabu. And even the very small percentage of those who maybe have eaten quite a lot of seaweed in their life, I would say none of them have eaten the kind of seaweed that we were serving them, let alone in the way that we were serving them. In the basket there were usually anywhere from five to eight varieties of seaweed. These might include young kombu, tosaka-nori, ryukyu-fudaraku, yumigata-ogonori, mizo-ogonori, mekabu, habanori, suji-aonori, yusuke sezaki. These you dipped. Then you have the smoked wakame stem in the broth and two different varieties of seaweed in the ponzu dipping sauce. So that was quite special for us. The fact that no matter how well-versed our guests were with seaweed and Japanese cuisine, we were able to give them a completely new experience that they haven't tasted before.

SHUI: The ponzu dipping sauce is made with sea buckthorn. That is obviously something that's quite common in Scandinavia and this was one of those things that in the past we were thinking there's no way that anybody has seen or grows sea buckthorn in Japan—but through our extensive research we were able to find one particular farmer who's based in Hokkaido and grows it. And this was a bit of a revelation because it meant that we were using Japanese produce, but with a distinct Nordic flavor to it.

METTE: Of course, it's harder now to work with seaweed in Copenhagen because of all the kinds we can't get there. It's problematic because we were spoiled by amazing variety.

> Even in Japan, with such a deep culture of eating seaweed, they only eat 50 to 100 types, meaning there's 1,400 varieties that have yet to make it on the plate.

SERVING NUMBER SEVEN

Cuttlefish with Whisky Vinegar

Thinly sliced cuttlefish marinated with whisky vinegar, dried roses and pumpkin bushi.

SHUI: The cuttlefish is a variety called mongoita. The flesh is extremely thick and it lends itself very well to be manipulated in a way where you can get these very thin slices out of it.

MIREK: We found it at Nishiki Market, from a fourth-generation fishmonger. It's really incredible. And we took it back and tried many variations. Served it warm and hot and then grilled. And actually we got pretty close with a grilled version but then when we tried it another couple of times—and none of us actually liked it. You have this beautiful thing and you're chasing the perfect texture. It's humbling. Humbling and annoying.

THOMAS: When we served it ice cold it was at first a bit chewy, almost an al dente pasta texture. As you started chewing it away, it just almost disappeared and melted in your mouth. And that's why the temperature was so important.

MIREK: Guests from the west, they don't appreciate textures as much as Japanese people. In Japanese, you have how many words for crispy? Seven or nine?

JUN: Yeah, it's a lot. Kari kari [crispy-crunchy], shaki-shaki [crunch-crunch]. The more chew something has, the fresher it seems to us.

MIREK: But in the west, if there's too much chew it seems like a cheaper product. We found that if the cuttlefish was served very cold it was super creamy but as it warmed to room temperature it was too chewy. At first this was going to be served in the basket as part of the hassun. We had it really cold and served on a leaf but it kept sliding everywhere. We were trying it again one day and it's sliding around and René asked me: "What are you thinking?" And I was like "I think it's stupid." [laughs] So chef asked Hiro who was walking by to bring us a big ice cube. He was like "Uh, yes chef." A minute-and-a-half later we had this giant ice cube. We took the cuttlefish very frozen from the freezer, marinated it quickly and then just put it on the ice cube. And as soon as we ate it off there, it was one of those moments in the testing phase that we all tasted it once, and we knew straight away this was it, we had to use it.

METTE: The test kitchen is always a team effort, but especially for this pop-up, it was so essential to have everyone's views on things. In Kyoto, we all kind of came with such different backgrounds. Thomas having had a restaurant in Tokyo and, of course we have Jun from Japan who has been with us for more than 10 years now. It was a really good mix of people who know so much about Japan, Japanese history, culture, food, everything, and then people for whom it is quite new.

SERVING NUMBER EIGHT

Shiro Ebi and Miso Crisp

Tiny white shrimp lightly marinated and served on a crisp of dried miso with peach tree sap.

SERVING NUMBER NINE
Bamboo Shoots in Squid Broth

Bamboo shoots cooked confit, thinly sliced, brushed with a paste of corn bushi and served in a broth of squid, jasmine and koji.

METTE: With the bamboo, we really wanted to find a way to cook it so we get the texture that we really love, where it's tender but still has a little bit of bite to it and still has that nuttiness.

JUN: First I did a very traditional cook for the group. Boiling the bamboo in rice bran water, then cooled in the liquid. If you don't cook in rice bran the bamboo leaves your mouth feeling itchy.

MIREK: We tried the bamboo a few different ways and then we thought maybe it'll work with cal, which is like the limestone you use in Mexico to nixtamalize corn, to break down the same sort of fibers. This ended up working really well.

METTE: Many dishes came together much, much faster than we are used to back in Copenhagen. Because we knew we wanted to give more focus to particular ingredients, for example, the bamboo-shoot serving. That was really beautiful and it was just the bamboo shoot and a clear squid broth with jasmine tea and koji oil. It still took a lot of time because we still had to cut down the bamboo and cook it and slice it. But I think that serving was about how to highlight the flavor and the texture of the bamboo and make it feel like noma. It's a format we've done before, these nutty, crunchy flavors paired with a really rich, but still clear and cold seafood broth. For the pop-up in Sydney, we had sliced macadamia nuts swimming in clear crab broth with rose oil.

We went to visit a bamboo farmer just outside Kyoto in the bamboo forest. And it was interesting because it's kind of like a semi-wild thing. And it's really only available in Kyoto in April. It's so crazy that to have this super seasonality where something is only available for one month. But I think it was quite inspiring for us, how they really respect the ingredients and highlight them for that short period of time that they're at their very best.

The first thing I did when I came home was to type into Google: bamboo, shoot, Denmark, eating. They're much thinner, the ones that grow in Denmark because of the weather, but I thought maybe it would be possible to eat the shoots as well. So the first article that came up was about a Danish Buddhist monk who had planted a bamboo forest around his temple. His idea was to grow bamboo shoots to supply restaurants. I got in touch with the monk who had then moved to the other side of the country. He wasn't there anymore, but the good thing was that the bamboo was still there. I also found another guy who is growing bamboo for the pandas in the zoo and let us pick some of his shoots. So, we ended up having bamboo shoots on the menu in Copenhagen this summer.

JUN: One special thing about Kyoto is how much tasting we did. In Copenhagen we are used to tasting every day between ourselves but in Japan we were tasting with René every day. A bit of stress! But it led to a crazy amount of productivity. There was no distraction for anyone and we were all working together in a small space. When we did tastings, the table was always completely covered in dishes and ingredients. But that messiness led to creativity. Sometimes you see two things and think, why not put them together? And sometimes it becomes something amazing. Not always, but sometimes [laughs].

In the bamboo forest it's a semi-wild thing... only available in Kyoto in April... this super seasonality where something is only available for one month.

SERVING NUMBER TEN

Swordfish Belly

Raw swordfish belly with a rich sauce of butter and kelp.

THOMAS: In Japan, swordfish belly is not really visible as an ingredient. So, we were talking to a sushi chef and Shui was translating. Why wasn't it a popular cut?

SHUI: In most cases you would never find a sushi restaurant that would serve swordfish belly and we, as outsiders, couldn't understand. Because we genuinely felt that the fat content, the clean flavor and the balance between the fat and the flesh of this cut was just as good if not better than tuna belly, which is like arguably the most revered cut of raw fish you can get in Japan. We asked some local chefs, and this could just be their view, but they explained there was an aesthetic element always to be considered when you're choosing what fish to use for sushi and tuna belly has this luscious looking pink color and shine that for the Japanese really makes their mouth water. If you look at swordfish belly, it's white flesh with white flat fat, just completely white. The aesthetics of this, we were told, were quite frankly very boring. Sometimes, he says, it's just as simple as that

THOMAS: We'd played around with swordfish belly in Tokyo and Australia so it was always at the back of our minds as something we'd like to try again. When we tried it here it was one of our favorite pieces. Then it became about figuring out what is the right temperature of the fish. How cold or warm does it need to be? How cold or warm does the sauce need to be? How warm or cold does a plate need to be? So, it all comes together and really becomes this perfect marriage of, in the end, two ingredients, kelp sauce and swordfish belly. The fish itself was served at room temperature and the sauce a little above body temperature, so around 40-42 degrees when it got to the table. That slightly warmer than body temperature gives a special sensation. The way it melts, it's it just adds a pleasurable sensation to the eating experience.

SERVING NUMBER ELEVEN
Tofu and Wild Almonds

Green soy tofu, a broth of koji and dashi, grated almonds, nasturtium flowers and marjoram oil.

SERVING NUMBER TWELVE

Kinki

A small redfish, shortspine thornyhead, found along Hokkaido and prized for its fattiness. Grilled over bintochan and finished with cured egg yolk sauce.

SERVING NUMBER THIRTEEN

Lotus Root

Whole lotus root cooked confit, then grilled low and slow over charcoal and glazed with truffle. Seasoned heavily with black pepper to finish and a clam butter sauce for dipping.

> You can't do it better than nature. All we can do is to try to understand a product, where it's coming from, when it is at its absolute finest.

SERVING NUMBER FOURTEEN
Sansai

Sansai is a term for spring mountain vegetables. A dish that started the sequence of the main course with various mountain vegetables cooked in different ways with a sauce from the head of ise-ebi (spiny lobster) that epitomizes spring in Kyoto.

THOMAS: The most important part of any research trip is that you need to go to a product or to a producer to experience it at its absolute finest. I still recall the best razor clam I've ever had was when we had a research trip in 2017 into the Arctic Circle of Norway, where Roderick Sloan dived to the bottom of the ocean and pulled up a razor clam and just gave it to me straight from the ocean. It was unforgettable, the sheer quality and flavor, the texture and the purity of the waters where it was coming from was incredible. And you can apply an experience like this to a tomato or to a perfect peach picked in late summer from the tree when it's perfectly ripe. You can't do it better than nature, in my opinion. The only thing that we can do is to try to really understand a product, where it's coming from, when it is at its absolute finest, why is it at its absolute finest, and what is happening in between. Someone takes it off the vine, off the tree, or pulls it out of the soil and brings it to us. How can we make sure that the quality of the product declines the least possible way?

Then from the experience of those research trips, we can think: what is it now we as a chef need to do to get as close as possible to that moment? I think the easiest way to be inspired is just look around you. You know, you pick a tomato and there's some kind of sorrel growing next to it on the ground and maybe some chamomile. Look at nature and let it guide you. I think it's really simple sometimes; allow yourself to be extremely open-minded beyond that one thing why you went to this farm or to a place.

SERVING NUMBER FIFTEEN
Ise-ebi

The main course, Japanese ise-ebi (spiny lobster), quickly steamed, then finished over bintochan. Dressed with a paste of corn bushi, pumpkin bushi, and kihada berries. Sancho leaves on top and sudachi to the side.

METTE: The paste of corn and pumpkin bushi was the most amazing condiment ever. You could just sense straight away that it would be really beautiful to pair it with red shellfish. It adds a whole new kind of flavor that we haven't really worked with before. The paste itself was brushed onto the bottom of the ise ebi tail, and then extra pumpkin bushi was grated on top of the paste. The tail was served upright, so the guest couldn't see the paste or the pumpkin bushi, so the crazy layers of flavor became an unexpected surprise, but for some reason familiar to noma.

THOMAS: The work on the pumpkin bushi and corn bushi goes back to 2017, between old and new noma, when we were working in the kitchen at René's house. He asked us to start working on different types of katsuobushi, without using bonito and we didn't really succeed. Later at Inua we took up the project again because now we were in the motherland of katsuobushi. And we had an incredible supporter and collaborator, a katsuobushi maker in Kagoshima, who was willing to risk his reputation and just try unheard of, completely crazy things.

METTE: The flavor of katsuobushi is everywhere in Japan. It's one of the signature flavors of the country.

THOMAS: Katsuobushi might seem simple, but it's not at all simple. First you start with the fish, the way it's been butchered, the way it has been trimmed, also how fast or slowly it has been processed. Then how do you steam it, where do you steam it, when do you steam it? And then there's the entire drying process/smoking process. How long and what kind of smoke? How hot is it? How cold is it outside? Is it raining? The humidity? How do you apply the mold so it can dry not too fast, not too slow, so it doesn't get infected with a different mold. How long do you age it? Where do you age it? You see the variables are huge and I probably haven't even pointed out 20 percent. So this is one reason to work with a traditional producer. Another is that we want to be inspired by Japan and by its people and by its culture and just to see it with a new and fresh eye.

So we sent everything and anything we could find in the market. Quince, pears, apples, lotus root, carrots, cucumber, radishes, turnips. And then it just happened that pumpkin bushi came first and then corn bushi. Those two were just the tastiest of it all. Bloody trial and error! The gentleman we are working with, he's incredible. He thinks so differently and so much deeper and more diversely about one particular thing we only see from afar.

METTE: When you taste it, it's like, wow, that really feels like a flavor in our universe. And it makes you ask, where does this flavor belong? Because it's not Danish, that's for sure. And it's not really Japanese either. It's like some weird in-between. Something about the smokiness reminds me of chillies that feel almost more Mexican than Japanese.

SERVING NUMBER SIXTEEN
Green Rice with Roses

Green rice cooked with wild rose oil, seasoned with rose vinegar, fresh rose petals and cherry shoots. Served with trimmings from the isi-ebi.

SHUI: We knew we wanted to incorporate rice as an ingredient at some point in the menu because rice is a staple in Japan. We tested many different kinds, starting with white. But we really, really wanted to do something to take it somewhere that it hasn't been before.

We were in a group meeting and I said, "How would you feel if I were to bring in a sample of green rice?" This was interesting, because a lot of people had never heard of green rice before. Green rice isn't unripe or picked early. It's an ancient variety that grows green to maturity. Before white rice was a staple all around the world, we had red rice, green rice, black rice. These heirloom varieties have mostly died out.

We did many, many tests on how to cook the green rice. It's very different than white. From the amount of water you use, the time you wash it, the amount that you let it steep in the water, to the way it tastes at the very end is all incredibly different. It's much nuttier, more textural, more of a chew to it.

THOMAS: It was eye-opening. We always approached it more as a grain serving rather than a rice serving, because as Shui said, the texture was something beyond. I mean, crunchy is the wrong word. But when you were eating it, it almost popped in your mouth. It wasn't this soft, creamy thing. There was like a real chew to it, which was really, really refreshing.

SHUI: This combination just speaks of the season most eloquently. The fact that it's this rice with flowers, roses in particular, but flowers, and the pop-up was there in Kyoto in the spring. It was just a fragrance, it was like a visual thing and a textural thing too. All of this in that moment in time just made the most sense. And by the wild cherry shoots, we mean the very, very first young tender leaves that kind of sprout from the branches during spring.

THOMAS: The flavor of those: imagine bitter almond flavor from the forest.

SHUI: Yes. This might not be helpful for anyone not well versed in the way that we cook, but if you know pine to be the flavor of the forest during autumn and winter, then these wild cherry shoots to us in Japan are what the forest tastes of in spring and summer.

SERVING NUMBER SEVENTEEN

Yuzu Shijimi Clams

Tiny "clams" stuffed with yuzu sorbet with sake gel, plum kernel oil and yuzu zest.

METTE: Shijimi are the kinds of clams you classically get in miso soup at sushi restaurants. The idea was to have a bowl of clams but as a dessert. It ended up being like a shell made from cream with a bamboo ash, with yuzu sorbet inside.

JUN: The basic idea comes from traditional Japanese sweets called wagashi. Some shops make wagashi in the shape of a clams, but the shell is not edible, just the gum gel inside. So, we thought it's more fun if you can eat the whole thing.

MIREK: On our first research trip to Kyoto, these shijimi clams were one of the first items we picked up from the market. We had this kind of clam on the menu in Tokyo and it was an extremely difficult dish to execute. Really, we want to steer clear of these clams. But it was almost like we wanted to show the clams that we can do it [laughing]. We're going to show them by turning them into dessert. So the first day we were there, chef said, "Maybe we can make a clam ice cream." We were all like "Fuck that's cool!" And then we tried to work on it a little bit. We smuggled back some shells and we tried to work on it in Copenhagen. But when we got back to the space in Kyoto, we felt there's no way to make them into a dessert. It's too difficult. But then somehow Mette nailed it.

METTE: The technical challenge was how to make a whole bowl of clam shells per person? How is it even technically possible? We got a bunch of clams in and put them into silicone to make molds. We ended up making about 150 molds, each one could make about eight whole clams. We freeze the mold, paint it with cream and the ash to give it the appearance of a clam. Before we got to yuzu, we tried probably 30 different flavors—and then decided that we just love the flavor of yuzu with sake. It's not rocket science; these are flavors that you see together quite often in Japan. But it's also fun because when you bring it to the table the guests would be like "What is going on?"

SERVING NUMBER EIGHTEEN TO TWENTY
Petit Fours

Dried strawberry with cardamom caramel and mochi, eggfruit from Okinawa with elderflower, and sweet potato puree dipped in a shell of cherrywood oil with whipped cream on the side.

Extra Servings

Served in the event of dietary restrictions or if certain products were unavailable.

1. **Kyoto Carrot** – Fried and grilled Kyoto carrot served on a miso crisp

2. **Wild Boar Belly** – Grilled and glazed wild boar belly

3. **Grilled Enoki Mushrooms** – Grilled stems of enoki mushrooms with black truffles, pumpkin bushi, and sudachi.

4. **Ama-Ebi & Peas** – Sweet shrimp, spring peas, and a broth made of clams and tomato.

5. **Seaweed Soba** – Buckwheat noodles with aonori seaweed powder and a broth of smoked wakame stem and pine dashi.

6. **Citrus and Kelp** – Fresh pomelo with kelp oil and aromatic spices.

7. **Crispy Hirome Seaweed & Konatsu Dessert** – Sweet crispy seaweed, cream, and konatsu citrus.

8. **Sweet Koji Onigiri** – The very first version of a sweet koji onigiri that eventually became a dessert in Copenhagen. Koji wrapper, matcha and pumpkin-seed milk ice cream, huscup and ado berry reduction, koji glaze, all wrapped with sweet, crispy, hirome seaweed.

9. **"Koji" Birthday Cake** – Plum and sake sponge layered with rose-yuzu mousse, dried cherry blossoms, kiwi. Shaped like koji.

10. Top to bottom: pumpkin bushi, corn bushi, katsuobushi

1

3

2

4

5

- Hassun ***
  - Koji & Ginger — Jun
  - tomato & poken gel — Hi
  - cherry leaf — D.
  - Yuba & Ramson — T
  - tomato flower — ME

- Hot pot of seaweeds & vegetable
  ? DEVIL SHRIMP ?
- Cuttlefish sashimi
- Shrimp & peas
- Sword fish belly
- Squid broth & Bamboo
- tofu
- lotus steak **
- Kinki ***
- Sun seki ***
- ISE EBI ***
- Rice & Roses ***
- Crispy seaweed
- Clam dessert
- ~~mochi - citrus/cardamom~~
  POTATO + CREAM
  EGG fruit

Extras:
- Devil shrimp ***
- Birthday cake
- tokyo carrot flatbread
- White shrimp & tree sap flatbread

I processi:
- Soba
- ~~[crossed out]~~
- Onigiri dessert
- tempura
- Petit four ~~[crossed out]~~
  - sweet potato
- Dashi/Broth with tree sap

Noma Kyoto menu 2023

The finished menu of Noma Kyoto.

The Way of Fermentation

As in all cuisines, modernity, and tradition each have a place in kitchens. And the sublime ferments of Kyoto show that there is no single path to deliciousness.

TO EXPLORE gastronomy in Japan is not just to explore the cuisine of one single place, but to tug on common threads stretching across the globe, tethering techniques and ingredients utilized the world over to advance the pursuit of deliciousness. Western cuisine owes much of its prestige to the quiet, deliberate practices of Japan. Traces of Nippon decorate the 1960s advent of nouvelle cuisine, kaiseki built the foundation upon which the modern tasting menu stands, and even Ferran Adria, perhaps the most prominent exponent of modern avant-garde cuisine, credits his visits to Japan as inspirational treasure troves for El Bulli in Spain. Japan represents a unique paradigm shift in the way the world cooks, despite many practices remaining shrouded in mystery to outsiders. Like 40s and 50s era Kurosawa films inspiring subsequent classics such as *Star Wars*, *Kill Bill* and *The Magnificent Seven*, many so-called original ideas in cuisine are derived from the lengthy and rich history of Japan.

One of Japan's areas of provenance, and one of those tendrils that stretch across borders, is the expertise in fermentation. Though there are many cuisines in the world involving fermentation, only a small group shares the distinction with Japan of relative ubiquity across markets. Misos and shoyus are found with regularity in homes and restaurants far from their places of origin. While noma endeavours to celebrate the produce and practices of Scandinavia, the influence of Japan is woven heavily through the restaurant's identity. During our time in Kyoto, we were afforded the privilege of observing, experiencing and tasting the progenitors of so many methods and products that contribute to how we cook (and therefore who we are) at noma.

In gastronomy, few ingredients possess the mystical allure of koji. This ancient mold, scientifically known as *Aspergillus oryzae*, has been an intrinsic part of Japanese cuisine for centuries, transforming humble grains into a treasure trove of flavors and elevating dishes to new heights of culinary excellence.

Koji's history traces back to the earliest days of Japanese civilization, where its serendipitous discovery catalyzed the development of what would become Japanese cuisine. More than two thousand years ago, a fortuitous encounter occurred when a rice-filled container was inadvertently left in a warm, moist environment. Soon, a velvety white mold enveloped the rice, imparting an enchanting aroma and a delightful umami-rich taste.

Koji *(Aspergillus oryzae)* grown on rice in traditional wooden trays, often made from cedar

Over the centuries, koji production was gradually refined and eventually domesticated. Scientifically, the effect that aspergillus has on starches such as rice, soybeans, barley, and more has remained constant; armed with an arsenal of enzymes, including amylases and proteases, they break down starches and proteins into their constituent parts—glucose and amino acids, the heart of umami. The delicate balance of natural progression and human intervention over time yielded superior koji, enabling an entire civilization to build a culinary foundation that continues to support them centuries later.

Just outside central Kyoto stands Ikkyū-ji Temple, named for the master of Zen Ikkyū Zenshi who restored the temple after its destruction during the Genko war in 1331-1333. In addition to being a sacred ground for Zen Buddhism, the monks there produce and sell Ikkyū-ji natto, a variety exclusive to the temple produced by growing koji on soybeans and soaking them in a salt brine. The mixture is poured into wooden vessels and exposed to sunlight to gradually dry and reduce, resulting in a dried, blackened umami-rich sediment of chewy soybeans. The practice ensures that the monks will always have access to a delicious source of protein and also preserves the harvest of soybeans for off-season consumption. As with many ancient food practices, the monks of Ikkyū-ji Temple lament the fact that their style of natto is slowly disappearing from public knowledge, despite their best efforts to preserve this traditional food. We cannot overstate the privilege we received from these monks who opened their doors to us and shared their knowledge and techniques; walking the stone paths of the temple and seeing the old wooden vessels that house the drying soybeans was the closest to time travel we may likely ever experience. To see first-hand the production process of such an ancient and important product was memorable, to say the least.

Among the most sacred practices of the kaiseki tradition is the inclusion of shokuji—a course presenting perfectly steamed rice, a balanced miso soup and a bounty of pickles ranging from delicate to intense and governed by the seasons—that is served towards the end of the savory offerings. Intended to transition the diner elegantly into the sweet courses, these tsukemono are a representation of the exact seasonal moment a kaiseki ryori meal is being enjoyed. As the microseasons of Japan come and go, the pickles and ferments change and cycle as products mature and develop. We were lucky to be in Kyoto during the sansai, or mountain vegetable season when chefs scour the Kyoto countryside for wild foraged treasures.

While many of these sansai vegetables are served fresh, to celebrate the moment, a large amount is preserved, salted and fermented for later purposes, and to serve as tsukemono. Powerful, mouth-puckering umeboshi sidled up with delicate nuka-pickled cucumber and umami-packed squares of kombu pickle. Most memorably, to taste takuan in Japan after a lifetime of takuan being a salty, radioactive rod of MSG-gussied daikon jammed into a futomaki roll is to experience 4K resolution after a lifetime of NTSC. Markets heaved not only with several different qualities and maturities of takuan, but stalls offered seasonal tsukemono in a range of colours and flavors that make Baskin-Robbins' 31 flavors seem like a grain of sand in the Sahara. Part of market shopping in Japan was the perusal of fermented wares:

maybe this week the salted sakura are finally perfectly ripe, but the kasuzuke turnip greens are not quite there... Pickle culture dominates both the professional and home kitchen in Japan. Opening the cupboards in a Japanese home and not finding a crock or jar of something deliciously developing was a rarity; in reality, one need not even look, as the host had likely already arranged a dish of their house pickles to offer proudly to weary visitors.

The first bowl of ramen in Japan was a sensory experience. Chewy noodles, tender pork and a broth that slid the gamut of fatty to clean, rich to light. A traditional accoutrement to a bowl of ramen is menma, a fermented and dried bamboo shoot. It took many of us a few tries to become accustomed to the potency of this classic ramen garnish. It was described as "smells like wet dog", "reminiscent of urine" and "barnyard-y" by a significant number of our group. Initial bowls of ramen at Ichiryu Manbai involved scarfing the menma as quickly as possible to avoid tainting the rest of the ramen experience with the unbearable funk. Over time and numerous visits, the distaste for fermented bamboo shifted to a more favorable disposition, no doubt aided by our inability to ask the chef to forgo the menma in our bowls (one of many hurdles presented by language barriers). Eventually many of us began to truly appreciate the sour funk and its interplay with the fortified chicken broth and pork belly that it would ride shotgun with. Perhaps menma represents a microcosm of our visit to Japan; culture shock and disorientation evolving to appreciation, respect and even a longing for the experience once it has ended.

In the Western world, so much energy is driven into the optimization of things: how to make cars faster, how to make phones smaller, how to make buildings taller. While no argument can be made against Japan's similar fascination with technology and modernism, and its advancements in industry, it remains simultaneously in tune with the parts of the culture that demand more time and a more methodical pace. In a country credited with creating the microprocessor and inventing 3D printing, among its greatest incongruities is that offices and labs are likely to use fax machines regularly.

Over a span of 48 hours, steamed rice will develop a white mold as the koji grows on the grains.

> While it is definitely advantageous to be able to track the parabolic curve of enzymatic efficiency in a garum-temperature gradient, we wonder if that ability pales in comparison to an eighth-generation shoyu producer's ability to determine the quality of a shoyu moromi by "the way it feels when you stir it".

Fermentation at noma has relied on technology in many ways for many years. Our lab is constructed with individual chambers offering customizable temperature and humidity settings. We use metrics to examine salt and sugar percentages and to analyze pH levels. Our ovens are programmable to increments of a single degree of temperature and a single percentage of humidity. In our eyes, the fermentation lab at noma is a sterling global example of fermentation possibilities and prowess. You may understand then, why we found it humbling to have the so-called best technology available to produce a ferment and being blown away by the quality of a similar ferment produced only with manual labor, generational expertise and natural processes. While it is definitely advantageous to be able to track the parabolic curve of enzymatic efficiency in a garum-temperature gradient, we wonder if that ability pales in comparison to an eighth-generation shoyu producer's ability to determine the quality of a shoyu moromi by "the way it feels when you stir it".

It was an inspiring moment to realize the differences between our production styles, how they both can result in high levels of quality like two roads ending up at the same destination. We use technology to dictate the ideal environment for our ferments while the Japanese reverse the mentality, and they embrace nature's unpredictability, accommodating for changes as they go. Koji cannot be produced in the summertime because it is too warm for the aspergillus spores to proliferate. Shoyus are seasonal and produced at the same time of year, creating a calendar of sorts in which fermentation dictates diet and even celebrations. Through this more observant disposition towards fermentation, we gained a new respect for nature's ability to create deliciousness. Maybe we don't have to control every aspect to create something special. Maybe, as Jeff Goldblum's Dr. Ian Malcolm wisely said, "Life finds a way".

| WORDS | KENNETH FOONG, HEAD CHEF | PHOTOGRAPHY | FRITZ BUZIEK |

CUTTING EDGE

A knife is never just a knife in a Japanese kitchen. Centuries of craftsmanship and metallurgical knowledge, dedication and precision have forged these finely balanced instruments into an art form.

A shoal of knives, sleek as sharks; each blade with its own unique recipe of steel.

1. Blades by Yoshihiro Funaki.

2. Akonosuke White Steel Gyuto.

3. The Damascus cladding on a knife by Takamura Hamono.

4. 65 layers of steel to make one blade from Takamura Hamono.

5. The thick spine of a Deba knife.

IT IS no secret that the Japanese are some of the finest craftsmen in the world. Their dedication to their discipline and the spirit of their craft extends far beyond what we can comprehend in the Western world. It is no surprise that Japanese knives have earned a well-deserved reputation as some of the finest cutting tools in the world. With a history dating back centuries, these blades embody a level of craftsmanship and artistry that is unparalleled. They are more than just culinary tools; they are symbols of precision, tradition, and culture.

Japan holds a unique position in Asia because it avoided complete colonization by Western forces during the colonial period that spanned from the 16th to the mid-20th century. In an era where numerous Asian countries fell under European colonial rule, Japan retained its autonomy and sovereignty during the Edo Period (1603 to 1867) when Japan was ruled by the Tokugawa shogunate and was closed off to the outside world. This autonomy birthed a distinctive perspective on the evolution of its cuisine and the tools integral to Japanese culinary practices. Beyond the realm of knives, the Japanese also have a plethora of specialized tools that contribute to the intricacies of Japanese culinary preparation.

While most of us find ourselves quite comfortable in kitchens across the Western world, the layout of Japanese kitchens can appear rather foreign to an unseasoned cook. Pots and pans bear unique shapes tailored to precise functions, wooden paddles with a lining of sharkskin, and wooden contrivances resembling relics from a medieval era might leave one perplexed.

During our time in Kyoto, we had the opportunity and privilege to learn a little more about these tools and their applications. Japanese cuisine imparts a significant lesson in the appreciation of diverse textures. The act of grating, for instance, extends into a cosmos of varying tactile experiences. While Western kitchens tend to embody a Swiss Army knife culture that favors a one-size-fits-all approach, Japanese kitchens embrace the opposite philosophy. It is common to encounter tools in Japanese culinary traditions that are meticulously designed for a single, distinct purposes and nothing more.

Consider the oroshigane grater, now a fixture in our kitchen. While many are acquainted with the Microplane zester or the unassuming box grater, the oroshigane grater transcends the simple act of peeling zest from citrus. Its finely polished copper surface, adorned with burrs, masterfully crafts an aromatic paste from the zest, extracting highly volatile oils released through these abrasive burrs. This intricate process remains beyond the reach of tools such as the Microplane.

Then we enter the realm of knives. The history of Japanese knives can be traced back to the time when Japan embraced metallurgy and started producing blades using the ancient technique of the tatara furnace. Initially, these blades were primarily used for warfare, but over time the focus shifted to culinary purposes. Japanese blacksmiths honed their skills, incorporating traditional techniques with innovations to create knives that were not only functional but also aesthetically pleasing.

Japanese knife-making is an intricate art form passed down through generations. Master blacksmiths spend years perfecting their craft, emphasizing the importance of creating blades with perfect balance, sharpness, and durability. Each knife is meticulously hand-forged, often using high-carbon steel, which ensures a sharp edge that retains its sharpness for extended periods.

While Western kitchens tend to embody a Swiss Army knife culture that favors a one-size-fits-all approach, Japanese kitchens embrace the opposite philosophy. It is common to encounter tools in Japanese culinary traditions that are meticulously designed for a single, distinct purposes and nothing more.

Choosing a blade

Selecting the ideal steel and blade configuration hinges on a blend of factors that encompasses your daily tasks and your familiarity with handling blades. The right choice can differ significantly based on these variables.

Most professionals tend to lean towards high-end stainless-steel knives (VG10, ginsan, powdered steel) for the bulk of their daily tasks. They would also have dedicated carbon-steel knives that they use for specific jobs, perhaps a white steel deba for breaking down fish or a blue super steel yanagiba for precision slicing of proteins in service.

The stainless-steel workhorses afford the convenience of switching seamlessly from tasks to task without having to pay too much attention to how ingredients would behave when coming into contact with the reactive carbon steel.

It's worth noting that the stainless-steel duo of a quality 210mm gyuto and a 150mm petty knife can capably tackle nearly any culinary endeavor. Combine this versatility with the knack for honing and maintaining a keen edge, and you've got yourself the most formidable arsenal in a chef's toolkit.

A Deba, good for breaking down fish or meat.

Deba

This sturdy, thick-bladed knife is used primarily for fish and meat butchery, as well as breaking down small bones.

Gyuto

The Japanese equivalent of a chef's knife, the gyuto is a versatile, all-purpose knife used for slicing, dicing, and chopping a wide range of ingredients. It is perhaps the most versatile knife and one most chefs will own.

Sujihiki

The western style equivalent of a yanagiba slicer. It has a double-sided edge that excels in slicing tasks.

Nakiri

The nakiri is a vegetable knife with a single beveled, straight, thin blade, which is perfect for precise vegetable preparation including julienne and chiffonade cuts.

Usuba

Another vegetable knife, the usuba is a double beveled knife that has a flat, thin blade which allows for fine cutting and precision work. The shape is often similar to a nikiri blade.

Yanagiba

Often used by sushi chefs, the yanagiba is a long, thin knife with a single-edged blade designed for slicing raw fish with precision. However, we have grown used to using it as an all-purpose slicer, especially in different blade lengths.

Petty

While, not strictly speaking, a traditional Japanese knife, it has grown in popularity even in Japanese cooking circles. The petty knife is a small general-purpose knife used for more nimble styles of slicing and dicing that is generally too cumbersome for the larger gyuto.

Santoku

A popular all-purpose knife, the santoku typically has a shorter, rounder blade than the gyuto. It excels at the rocking style of slicing, dicing, and mincing, making it a favorite among home cooks.

The craftsmanship of layered steel.

Types of steel

Within the expansive realm of Japanese knives, a diverse array of materials contributes to the crafting of blades, but there are two main categories: carbon steel and stainless steel.

STAINLESS STEEL

Stainless steel is an alloy that contains more than 12 percent chromium, a crucial addition that significantly bolsters its resistance against corrosion. However, the label stainless steel encompasses a vast spectrum of steels, spanning from molybdenum steel to the increasingly popular VG-10 steel, and includes powdered variations such as R2.

The important consideration when assessing stainless steel knives lies in comprehending the specific attributes of the steel. These knives share similar merits and demerits with their carbon steel counterparts; the higher the steel's hardness, the greater its capacity to retain a refined edge. Yet, paradoxically, this heightened hardness renders the blades themselves more brittle and challenging to sharpen.

CARBON STEEL

Knives made from carbon steel, unlike their stainless counterpart, have few or no elements that reduce corrosion and they require more upkeep and maintenance. But carbon steel is much harder than its stainless counterpart, which means it can create a finer edge and has better edge retention. However, the hardness can mean it's harder to sharpen, its brittleness causes more chipping, and it's less durable in terms of impacts. The reactivity of carbon steel can be annoying when working with ingredients with high acidity or alliums that might discolor.

Within carbon steel there are two main categories: blue steel (aogami) and white steel (shirogami).

Blue steel is the choice material in terms of high-end carbon steel knives, mainly due to their balance between hardness (a higher carbon percentage) and better resistance to corrosion.

White steel is identical to blue steel with the addition of chromium and tungsten. It is a pure form of carbon steel and is known to be very hard. It can be ground to a razor's edge but it is far more prone to corrosion.

Some tasks in the Noma Kyoto kitchen and the various knives used

1. **SLICING BAMBOO**
   Takamura, Hana Series, petty, 150mm

2. **PORTIONING OF SEAWEED**
   Aritsugu, VG10, gyuto, 210mm

3. **FABRICATION OF KINKI**
   Jikko, Hakugi, Shirogami 2, deba, 150mm

4. **SLICING WILD BOAR BELLY**
   Takamura, Hana Series, sujihiki, 270mm

5. **SLICING SWORDFISH BELLY**
   Yagihouchou, Shirogami 1, yanagiba, 240mm

Yagihouchou

Just off the beaten path of Nishiki market lies a quaint little store that is has been making knives since 1854. It has been owned by generations of women and has come to supply Kyoto with some of their finest wares and blades.

Yagihouchou has its factories in Sakai in Osaka like most of the knife makers in Japan, but you can find a very wide collection of both traditional Japanese knives along with western styles. They also have a beautiful selection of copper wares and various other kitchen tools.

Aritsugu

One of Japan's oldest and most prominent knife makers. It is currently run by the 18th generation of the family since its inception in 1560. Conveniently located in Nishiki Market, they carry both western and Japanese styles of blades in various materials and lengths. It gets a little crowded especially during peak tourist season, but it is certainly worth a visit.

Jikko

The fusion of traditional Japanese fine craftsmanship with contemporary packaging gives birth to a remarkable collection by Jikko. Their range of knives boasts both stunning beauty and sought-after allure, showcased within meticulously curated showrooms. A visit to their showroom on the east side of Kyoto, nestled in Pontocho, unveils a captivating assortment. Showrooms in Tokyo and Osaka further extend the opportunity to immerse oneself in their artistry. Jikko's collection spans a spectrum, catering to diverse preferences and budgets. From accessible stainless-steel pieces to the opulent honyaki blades gleaming with a mirror-polished sheen, their offerings are as varied as they are exquisite. Tradition finds a harmonious blend with innovation as Jikko showcases not only conventional pieces but also captivates with their more flamboyant creations. These eye-catching marvels may feature bone and ivory ferules, turquoise inlays and an array of distinctive blade finishes. Of course, exotic wooden handles stand as a testament to their penchant for the extraordinary.

INSTAGRAM
Tenderizing mushrooms for sashimi

Takamura Hamono

While not confined to Kyoto's bounds, it would be remiss not to mention the masterpieces crafted by the three Takamura brothers based in Echizen, a journey of approximately two hours from Kyoto. Terukazu is the oldest brother and is also the smith. My admiration for Takamura spans more than a decade, and their knives stand as unrivaled gems in my experience. Most of their knives are based off a R2 powdered steel core clad with varying steel types in the series.

Takamura blades are known to feature wafer-thin profiles and steep grind angles that can hold razor sharp edges for a long time. They are however quite difficult to come by; some of their higher quality series have a lead time of two to three years. Yet, the moment you cradle one of their blades, an epiphany occurs; why they hold the distinction of being among the most coveted blades globally.

A pilgrimage to Takamura Hamono is a trip that every chef should make at least once in their life.

To create the beverage program for Noma Kyoto, head sommelier Mees List crossed Japan, from the vines of Hokkaido in the north to the distilleries of Kyushu in the south, whipping through the landscape on bullet trains and winding slowly through the mountains on a local coach car. The travels resulted in an all-Japanese selection of drinks, from sake to wine, tea, beer, and whisky. They were also a whirlwind of meeting like-minded souls who took her drinking and eating all the good stuff. Through each of the eight pairings created for the menu, Mees relates stories of encounters with the prolific community of farmers, brewers, bartenders and baristas she met during her three-month research. Need some goat cheese in Hakodate? Want to know the best wine shop in Yamanashi? Where to eat the best Chinese food in Tottori? Need a legendary wine bar in Toyama? You know who to call.

Have Palate — Will Travel

In search of the perfect pairing

NOMA IN KYOTO

JANUARY 15, 2023

"In the last few days I've come again to the realization of the daunting task lying before us in creating this menu. Sitting here in our future dining-room space, I've been making seemingly endless lists of things I need to do, want to do, want to know, do not know, should get to know, need to solve, need to invent. By now I'm swimming in scribbled paperwork. Slowly though my thoughts are gathering, and appointments are being made so hopefully this brain soup will start to make sense sooner rather than later. The chefs are making long hours already in the kitchen, busily coming up with different techniques and I try not to walk in there too often—the air of concentration is so thick you can cut it with a knife."

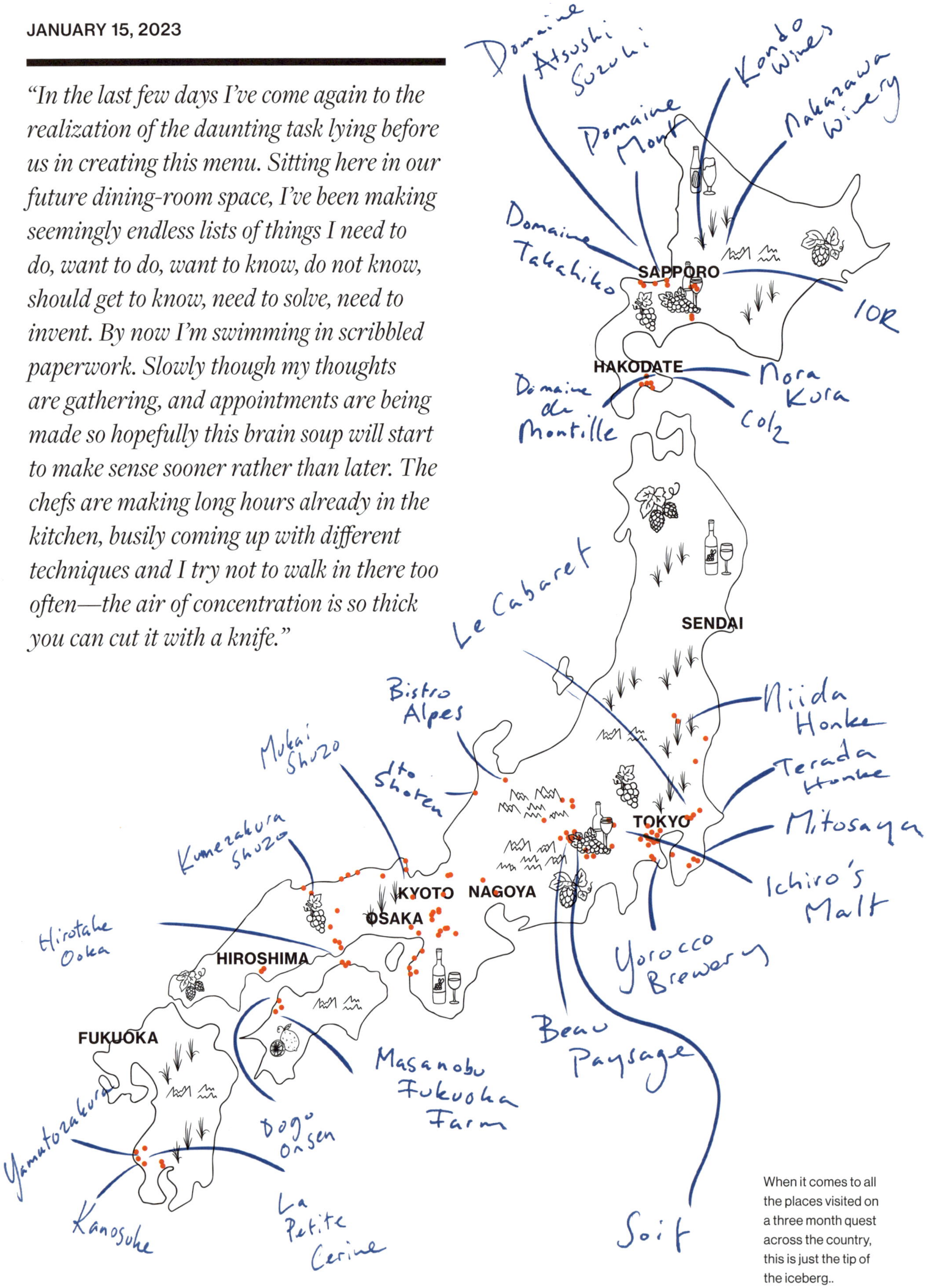

When it comes to all the places visited on a three month quest across the country, this is just the tip of the iceberg..

WHAT DOES IT MEAN to be the head sommelier at noma for a pop-up in Japan? Good question. I asked myself the same thing as I sat mile-high and wide awake, flying over the North Pole on my first visit to Japan, while the rest of the plane was either fast asleep or watching *Fast and Furious Part Godknowswhat*. It was about a year before we would open our doors to the first guests. Where to start as a foreigner in a country steeped in an age-old tradition of sake-brewing and tea-farming? How to convince natural winemakers so small and sought-after that getting hold of just a single bottle feels like a quest for the golden fleece, to sell us enough to serve on a pairing? One thing I knew for sure: I was going to try, come hell or high water, to only use Japanese products.

It was a gargantuan task to find the appropriate drinks for the event particularly before the menu was even created. There were wonderful guides along the way, chief among them Egami-san of the famous Kyoto wine shop Ethelvine, and Terada-san, the 24th-generation sake toji (head brewer) of Terada Honke. Both accompanied me on most of the road trips. And when they were not around, there was always Google Translate.

SOME WINE BARS NOT TO BE FORGOTTEN ACROSS JAPAN

LA PETITE CERINE, KAGOSHIMA
On the southernmost tip of Kyushu, find this fantastic wine bar with an amazing selection and a Parma ham from Gifu because why not.

BISTRO ALPES, TOYAMA
Owner Zac deejays behind his zinc bar, meanwhile pulling out some absolute gems from the cellar (and sometimes pulling off his shirt, depending on how crazy the night gets).

LE CABARET TOKYO
We cannot really skip Tokyo and in Shibuya be sure to visit the iconic Cabaret and the even more iconic Tsubo behind the bar.

LA PIOCHE, TOKYO
Get ready to blind taste wines with restaurant industry types from all over the world that visit this illustrious joint run by the knowledgeable and joyous Shinya. Also get ready to get stuck until the sun comes up and make your way home while the rest of the city commutes to work.

LEMON STAND, HIROSHIMA
Local oysters and Japanese natural wine, as well as a few other things from Europe. Also, incredible sausages made by a local man called Dotcomm.

SLOW CAVE, OKAYAMA
Great store with in the back a small bar area where you can drink Pedres Blanques rosé and eat delicious olives.

ITO SHOTEN, KANAZAWA
After spending an afternoon at say, the 21st Century Museum of Contemporary Art, or better yet the D.T. Suzuki Museum, and having lunch at the Ōmichō Market, go sit at the counter at Ito Shoten. Great winelist, cool records, wonderful host! Snacks too–you will need a double portion of the cheese.

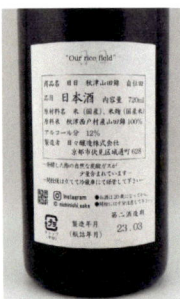

SAKE
2023 Our Rice Field

Hidehiko Matsumoto
Nichi Nichi, Fushimi, Kyoto

ACCOMPANYING DISHES
Hassun

WHEN you visit a sake brewery, as in many places in Japan, you go through the kerfuffle of changing shoes into slippers and into different slippers each step of the way. To prevent cross-contamination of all the yeasts and bacteria many breweries make you change from one pair where they wash and steam the rice, to another where the koji spores are cooking up, and yet another for the fermentation tanks and the press.

We are in Fushimi, the sake brewery district in the southern part of Kyoto, to visit Nichi Nichi. This brewery is run by Hidehiko Matsumoto, a young hip guy and 10th-generation toji who started his own shuzo a stone's throw from where his family once started. It is exactly two months before we open for a ten-week stint in this marvelous city, and I am looking for the perfect all-round sake, preferably as locally sourced as possible. The brewery is a small one: Nichi Nichi produces only three sakes, from three different fields. Looking for terroir in sake is not very common; most breweries buy their rice from various farmers and numerous areas, but Matsumoto is dedicated to an approach that seems more familiar to winemakers than sake toji. Instead of focusing on polishing rate, he tries to bring forth the flavor of the origin. As we conclude our tasting, upstairs in an old warehouse decked out with a hi-tech record player, enormous speakers and his grandfather's collection of analog cameras, Matsumoto makes us matcha. I think about the intersection of his sake with wine and ask him if he does blind tastings of sakes as sommeliers do with wines to train our capability to taste the source as well as the variety, and he nods in agreement. If only more breweries made rice from single fields.

Two months later, the full team arrives and with the week of preparations in full swing, all our waiters visit the brewery to understand firsthand how sake is made. As they change into plastic slippers and walk up the stairs, one person turns around and nudges her colleague: all our shoes have been swiftly reversed and neatly aligned for when the tour is over. It is a small gesture that makes the visit not only a lesson in sake-making, but also an eye opener about Japanese hospitality.

PAIRING ON THE MENU

We start the menu by pairing Our Rice Field—a testament to where we are—together with the hassun, the traditional opener of a kaiseki meal. A sake from the rice field owned and worked on by Matsumoto himself in summertime, made in tiny amounts, meticulously hand-labeled, that holds its own throughout all the different flavors and textures that come with the opening of the menu.

BEER
2023 Umi Yama

Akio Kichise
Yorocco Beer, Kamakura, Kanagawa

ACCOMPANYING DISHES
Seaweed Shabu Shabu

DRIVING into Kamakura, the temple-laden city south of Yokohama, the light changes to a friendly yellow and in the driveways, wetsuits hang drying: there is no doubt that Kamakura has replaced its shoguns with surfers. And where else but a surf town would you find a thriving craft beer scene? Yorocco Beer was founded in 2012 by local Akio Kichise on the northside, after he spent many years working at legendary underground club Oppa-la in Enoshima. His minutely crafted beers are marked by their subtle flavors and are hugely popular with fellow brewers and connoisseurs. At Yorocco, some brews are made with a local barley from the peninsula on the southern part of the Kanagawa prefecture. Finding barley in a rice-growing country is difficult, the reason why Japanese whiskies and beers are almost always made from foreign-bought grains. The perfect place to start a collaboration and brew a beer together.

"Can I come fishing for the wakame?" We have just made a game plan for the beer we want to make for the Kyoto pop-up: a light saison with a low-alcohol percentage, something you can drink at any point of the evening. The main added ingredient, we agreed, should be wakame seaweed. Seaweed is fished off the coast of Kamakura and it is also an often-used ingredient in the noma kitchen as a flavor maker bringing salinity and umami. We will balance the seaweed with a bergamot-like citrus and a wild-foraged mountain pepper picked by our friend Hiroshi Eguchi of Mitosaya Distillery.

Akio, Yorocco's owner and head brewer, raises his eyebrow at this unusual question but replies, "Yeah... sure." The 46-year-old reacts stoically at first to most of my proposals, but when he smiles it is genuine and with his whole heart. And so, three months later, I am hoisting myself into a pair of sturdy fisherman's pants on a brisk but not cold February afternoon in Zushi, one village over from Kamakura, about to step onto a boat so small there's only room three people and an empty bucket. The wakame season has just started and our fisherman is happy to take us on this unusual harvesting trip. Across the water the distant Mount Fuji solemnly observes our mission as we head off to the fishing nets in search of our bounty. Half a bucket seems sufficient for our needs and the next day we boil the seaweed into a dashi which we will eventually add to the already brewed saison. "What are we doing?" Akio laughs, "Are we making soup, or beer?" We continue to taste the broth until we feel like it has enough strength to add to the base beer. A mere 6 liters to 1,000 liters of beer makes a delicate flavor and a thirst-quenching drink.

PAIRING ON THE MENU

I never thought a beer would make the pairing, but once I tasted the seaweed shabu shabu, I knew this would be the best match. Be honest: what do you want to drink along with a steaming hotpot? Surely, it's a fresh brewski.

LOCATION TIPS

VANA VASA
A craft-beer bar and shop with everchanging beers on draft from Yorocco but also other great local breweries like Passific Brewing. Also a gallery with a regularly changing exhibitions. Beware of the dog! That fluffy little shiba munchkin likes to snap.

SO SAN
Next door to Vana Vasa is this wonderful wine bar with an impressive range of empty Beau Paysage natural wine bottles lining the top of the space. Simplicity is key here and the food is delish.

YOROCCO PUB
Go drink Akio's beer at the source. It's small, but that goes without saying with anywhere in Japan.

WINE

2019 Chardonnay

Eishi & Mayuko Okamoto
Beau Paysage, Hokuto, Yamanashi

ACCOMPANYING DISHES

Cuttlefish, Shiro Ebi, Bamboo Shoots, Swordfish Belly

BEAU PAYSAGE, on the north side of Yamanashi, not too far from Nagano, is about as appropriately named as they come. The vineyards are bathed in golden sunlight on a late November afternoon as we listen to Eishi Okamoto, speaking with sparkling eyes, avidly gesturing and walking through the vines that have begun to turn from green to bright reds and yellows. The patches of his vineyard are interspersed with plots of vegetables and apple orchards belonging to his neighbors, and in the background we see the snowy tops of the Yatsugatake Mountains. To make wine in Japan, you need to escape the humidity by going up either in altitude or latitude, the reason both Yamanashi and Hokkaido have become the epicenters of the country's nascent wine culture. Okamoto grows mostly merlot and chardonnay, along with a handful of grape varities including cabernet franc, pinot gris and a few Nebbiolo plants. A few years into his venture he decided to uproot most of his vines to face not north-to-south, as they do in many places in the world, but east-to-west, so the grapes have the longest exposure to sunlight throughout the day, which he believes in strongly.

A legend in Japanese winemaking, Eishi started his small three-hectare domaine in 1999 and has been an example for many winemakers across the country, and only sells his wines to a select handful of restaurants. A supporter of many good causes, his gentle character is exemplified by the words printed on the back of each of his wines, paraphrasing Lennon: "A glass of wine can change the world. Yes, we can change the world if we change our daily food and drink. You may think I am a dreamer, but I hope someday you will join us."

It is just days after the last harvest, and after our walk through the vines we spend the evening in the home of Eishi and his wife Mayuko tasting the wines as they lay out a cheese platter made by Okayama-based Yoshida Farm (best caciocavallo east of Italy), singing songs from *The Sound of Music* with their two children who go to an international school, and playing *Black Radio* by Robert Glasper. But as midnight comes around, Eishi and Mayuko disappear to the cellar to carefully rack the grapes which have just started fermenting, and then quietly the night comes to an end.

LOCATION TIPS

SOIF HOKUTO

A small wine shop in a building shaped like a tiny modern art museum right by the Nagasaka station. This cellar has a great selection of wines not often seen in the bigger cities, where the rare stuff quickly gets snatched away, as well as some wonderful sour beers and dry goods. A good place to stock up before a picnic and swim in the nearby waterfalls at Ojiragawa Canyon.

TERASAKI COFFEE

Wonderful coffee roaster and shop in the center of Kofu. Better yet, they have a second location in the woody outparts of Hokuto sited in yet another wildly spacy architectural construction, with fantastic pastries and charming staff.

PAIRING ON THE MENU

In my mind Beau Paysage not only produces the best wines in Japan, but some of the best in general, and his was the first Japanese wine I drank, almost a decade ago. As soon as I tasted the sauce from the swordfish belly, I knew it needed a fresh yet round chardonnay, and Eishi was kind enough to supply us with enough to serve during at least a big chunk of the noma pop-up. A real joy to be able to offer this hard-to-find wine to our guests.

SAKE
2023 Starbursts

Tomonari Miwa
Kumezakura, Maruyama, Tottori

ACCOMPANYING DISHES
Tofu and Wild Almonds

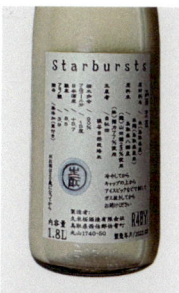

A FOUR-HOUR drive from Kyoto, north-west to the Sea of Japan sea, we meet Tomonari Miwa, head of the brewing process at Kumezakura. He is quite the exception in sake-brewer land: new to the game and, while the brewery itself has been around for over a hundred years, he started making sake here eight years ago after a previous career in fashion. Under his helm, Kumezakura has foregone all use of chemicals and eschews addition of yeasts to most cuvees. He is a tall and sturdy man with a wild bunch of hair, and though he speaks not a word of English, we have somehow found a way to communicate through a slew of poetic bot-translated emails back and forth, and in spring, with the pop-up well on its way, we are finally able to visit.

From the tenth floor of our hotel, we can see Mount Daisen on one side, the sea on the other, with not much but forest between. We make our way to the field where the rice is grown for the Starbursts. From the field, all we can see is the humongous volcano, and if it wasn't for our hotel sticking out from the trees, I'd feel like we're on the set of Jurassic Park, a flock of pterosaurs about to fly over the wild valley bordering the rice paddies below. Back at the brewery, Miwa's love for music is exemplified by the playlists he has drawn up by paintbrush by his kimoto-making room, where the process of making the yeast starter can be hard and monotonous, but The Jackson 5, the Gypsy Kings and AC/DC have helped lighten the workload.

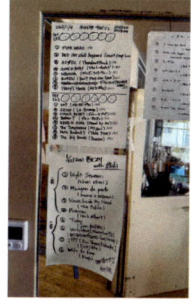

I first discovered Kumezakura in a small bar in Kyoto, where the labels immediately caught my eye; all hand-printed and painted beautifully and not so traditionally, from a large violet-like flower to a blue dinosaur, to a simple design of washi paper halfway dipped in indigo dye. It is clear that Miwa has a good eye for design and loves calligraphy. Even the samples of his new vintage that he sends to the Ace Hotel are accompanied by hand-painted explanations in beautifully drawn kanji, more evidence that we have found ourselves in a country with so much care for craft and detail.

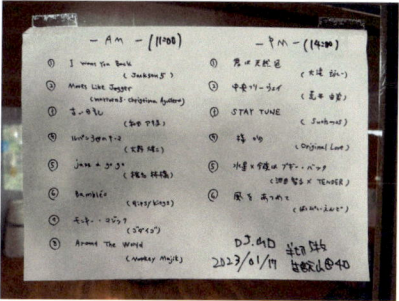

PAIRING ON THE MENU

Starbursts, a nigori sake with only ten percent of the grain polished off, tastes exactly like it sounds, explosive and otherworldly, the texture smoothing out the tingling touch on the tongue. Nigori sake means cloudy sake, and it is a style that is typical for winter brewing season. Bottled with a fair amount of rice bran and particles, it is drunk young and sometimes it can be quite wild, with its yeasts continuing to ferment, making it fizzy at times. Combined with the silky tofu, Starbursts is that little spoom in the middle of the meal.

LOCATION TIPS

HASSENKAKU
If you ever find yourself in Yonago, visit this wonderful little Chinese restaurant run by Naomi Mikami and her husband, who took over the place from his father. Amazing hospitality, delicious food, and of course, Kumezakura bottles everywhere.

WINE
2021 Dom Gris JK

Atsuo Yamanaka
Domaine Mont, Yoichi, Hokkaido

ACCOMPANYING DISHES
Kinki, Lotus Root

OH YOICHI! A small Hokkaido town led by a young enthusiastic mayor, famous for its Nikka Distillery and for its burgeoning wine scene. We have a big day ahead of us visiting no less than five winemakers who thankfully all pretty much live on the same road.

The first stop is Atsuo Yamanaka of Domaine Mont. Yamanaka originally came to Hokkaido years ago to be a snowboard instructor on its famous powder snow, and he still spends part of his winters on the slopes. We meet him by his winery where he only grows pinot gris grapes. Working as a sommelier when not standing on a board, he realized that he wished to make wine. He started his own domaine in 2016, planting about 1.5 hectares of pinot gris. In Hokkaido, Burgundy and Alsatian grape varieties tend to reign supreme, and there are fewer hybrids than I expected to encounter. Many wineries are small; to remain a legal alcohol-producing company (which in Japan means you must manufacture a minimum amount) many farmers need to buy grapes and make negociant wines to supplement their own production. Unfortunately, it is pretty much impossible to buy organically grown grapes in the region, as there is no incentive for most farmers to do so. It's an unfortunate situation for which there is no solution yet, but there are many new wineries starting in the area, and hopefully in the future there will be more motivation for others to commit to pesticide-free farms.

It is the first winery I have visited on this side of the world, and the wines of Yamanaka are impressive, especially the Dom Gris. Made from his own grapes, which he has vinified leaving the skins to macerate for a few weeks, the wine has a bright amber tint and a sharpshooting precision. It is at least five months before we open and the menu is far from being made, but I have no choice; this is the moment to decide which kind of wine I want to buy, before vintages get bottled and released to the general public. If I know the chefs in the test kitchen, this wine I know for sure will definitely fit at some point in the menu. So, there we are, standing, in the tiny warehouse, looking at the few barrels filled with wine. Any amount asked for seems like too much, and I am not familiar with Japanese dealmaking. But I do know one thing—if I never ask, nothing's going to happen. With a soft smile I look him in the eye. "It's so delicious. Would you possibly be able to sell us some?" Luckily for us, he smiles right back.

LOCATION TIPS

SAGRA
For those wanting to eat local, seasonal, inventive food and drink the wines of Yoichi, go to Sagra. In this restaurant, its charismatic chef Hiroto Murai simultaneously serves a tasting menu to each table while announcing what we're about to eat from behind his counter. At the end of the meal, he stands behind the wines that were served on the pairing, and in loving detail describes them to the guests. There's a wonderful bed and breakfast attached to the place; reservations go quickly.

KAKIZAKI SHOTEN
Right around the corner from the Nikka factory, on the first floor of a food market, check out this popular lunch place for a perfect rice bowl with super fresh seafood. I think about this rice bowl more often than you want to know.

PAIRING ON THE MENU

Thank the heavens, I think, as I take my first bite from the kinki fish covered in egg yolk sauce. It is pinot gris time.

SAKE	ACCOMPANYING DISHES
2023 Mori no Uta	Sansai

Masaru Terada
Terada Honke, Kozaki, Chiba

FEBRUARY 2ND 2023: *Today, I received the sample of the sake Terada-san made especially for our pop-up. I sat in front of this little bottle for about an hour before I tasted it, I was so nervous! But we can all rest assured, it is amazing. Sweet, acidic, so full of flavor and so well balanced, I can just imagine it to be so good with some bitter and roasted vegetable flavors of some sort.*

My knees hurt from trying to sit on the floor, but it doesn't matter. By now it is completely dark outside and the rain has started pouring down. Sitting under the high roof of the century-old tasting room at Terada Honke I have just gathered enough courage to ask Terada if he would be willing to collaborate on a sake for our Kyoto project, and he has agreed. I cannot believe the honor just bestowed on me and ignore a sleeping left leg while we discuss what kind of sake might work for our event. It is April 2022, three days since I first set foot in this country. I think it counts as a good start.

Earlier that day I stood in my first rice paddy, sneakers sinking into the mud, gazing at the vast expanse of plant life completely new to me, inhaling a forest smell that is fresh in every meaning of the word. This year, Terada tells me, will be the first time in ten years that rice has been grown here, so the soil is incredibly fertile. This field is surrounded by forest, which means that there is much water and it is untainted by neighbors' pesticides, something that can get in the way of trying to farm rice organically. Terada Honke (this year celebrating its 350-year anniversary), is internationally renowned as one of the very few sake breweries using only indigenous yeast and organically grown rice, a very rare thing in a country where organic farming is pretty much non-existent. Terada, who married into the family, taking its name as his own, now counts as the 24th-generation brewer of the house, and has been the head for more than twenty years. It was his father-in-law who felt opposed to the post-war industrialization that had taken over the country's agriculture and decided to return to the sake making of yore, for which his brewery was already equipped. To this day not much machinery is found inside the ancient building, and from the fields to the koji room most labor is done by hand.

Months later, back in Copenhagen, I receive a message from Terada, writing that he wants the first harvest from that very rice field we stood in, to be the base for our collaboration sake. "I know you noma people like to forage. I have been thinking about throwing some acorns from the surrounding forest into the sake." Hey—why not?

PAIRING ON THE MENU

The resulting sake, which we name Mori no Uta (Song of the Forest) has a distinct sweetness to it—so sweet that I initially think maybe it should accompany a dessert. Until I remember the bitterness of the mountain vegetables and I know exactly where it belongs.

LOCATION TIPS

CAFÉ UFUFU
Satumi Terada, Masuru's wife and the actual 24th generation of the Terada family, runs a small, mostly vegan café next door to the brewer. It's open only a few days a week; "Business days irregular", says the website. She uses the sake lees and koji from the brewery to marinate and ferment the tasty lunch dishes.

TSUKI NO TOFU
Across from Terada Honke is a famous shop making tofu from local organic soybeans. Make sure you come early, since they sell out most of their goods every day before noon.

WINE

2020 Kaze

Bruce & Ryoko Gutlove
10R Winery, Iwamizawa, Hokkaido

ACCOMPANYING DISHES

Ise-ebi, Green Rice with Roses

WAY UP in Hokkaido in a small place named Iwamizawa, we find 10R Winery, run by Bruce and Ryoko Gutlove. Their tiny 1-hectare plot is divided into two fields, one with white grapes, Mori, which means forest, for its proximity to the trees, and one with red grapes named Kaze, which means wind. It is October and this field lives up to its name; the wind seems to cut straight through my winter coat and the famous Hokkaido snow has not even begun to fall. Every year about two meters of snow cover the vines for months, a kind of blanket protecting them from the harsh temperatures. Ryoko seems quite unfazed by the wind as she stands tall, prune cutters in hand. Because of the snow, pruning begins right after harvest ends to get some work done before the vines are completely buried for months.

As small as the vineyards are, the winery itself is immense and still being expanded, as it serves as a learning facility for the many enthusiastic young winemakers starting out in Hokkaido. They can use the machinery, from presses to pumps, as well as the vessels and storage space for their wine. Becoming a winemaker is not easy and equipment is expensive, but the most important thing is to get advice. Bruce has been in the field for decades, from California back in the day, and has spent almost 40 years in Japan, first as the winemaker for Coco Wineries, and since 2012 here in Iwamizawa. Easy to talk to, he clarifies that he does not prescribe to others how to make their wine but rather he is there to help them during the process. He speaks of influential travels many years ago, visiting natural wine makers in Europe and how important the community is. All around us aspiring vintners are busy cleaning their tanks and ranging tools neatly sorted on the walls, creating a lively atmosphere unexpected in this gusty town. Japan is still very much at the beginning of its journey in wine, figuring out which grape varieties work best on its soils and in its climate, and at 10R they are trying out different cultivars on their small plots of land, including for instance the wildly popular poulsard and savagnin from France's Jura region. Visiting 10R you sense the future of wine in Japan is bright–and breezy.

LOCATION TIPS

AJIDOKORO
A traditional Kaiseki restaurant where the chef comes out wearing an apron he made himself from centuries old cloth, where the food is astounding and the beer served cold.

TOKUSA
Tokusa is a small izakaya in Sapporo with an amazing natural wine list, many of them local. Our hostess served us wine in the most outrageous collection of vessels, from hand-painted Murano glass to bamboo beakers to wildly shaped flutes. I'd say go just for the variety of beautiful glasses alone, but there is so much more to this wonderful little restaurant/bar.

PAIRING ON THE MENU

The Kaze 2020, made from primarily pinot noir with some gamay, pinot meunier, and poulsard to finish, was probably my favorite wine of the entire Hokkaido trip. Floral and fresh, it was perfect with the fleshiness of the ise-ebi lobster and the roses in the rice dish.

WINE
2022 Citrus Mix

Hirotake Ooka
Masanobu Fukuoka Farm, Iyo, Ehime

ACCOMPANYING DISHES
Yuzu Shijimi Clams, Petit Fours

ON THE WALK into the forest, the presence of Masanobu Fukuoka looms suddenly in the shape of an enormous construction of tree trunks forming an outdoor stage, now long abandoned. His grandson Hiroki, now in charge of the farm, explains that 40 years ago this platform amid the tall trees was the site of gatherings, seminars and lectures. We walk on and not far from the podium, stands a house falling apart, half overgrown and sunk into the earth. Through the broken windows sunlight shines on the sink with deserted pans, and wooden beams puncture a rolled-up mattress. After his death aged 95, Fukuoka's family has decided to give his house in the woods back to nature and over time the construction will gradually become completely wild. For now, it's a strange almost voyeuristic look into one man's life.

Masanobu Fukuoka was a citrus and rice farmer in Ehime, on the northwestern part of Shikoku Island. His 1974 manifesto *The One Straw Revolution*, on do-nothing farming and consumer behavior has greatly influenced many agrarians, notably natural wine makers (as well as a certain red-headed sommelier here on a pilgrimage). In the book he pleads with farmers to stop using pesticides, to quit tilling and to follow the cycles of nature without interfering too much. He makes a convincing argument and his philosophical writing on consumption is inspiring and au courant. Hiroki Fukuoka tells me that over the last few years, he has had more visits from foreign vignerons than rice farmers; there are not many people trying to grow rice organically, but he remains hopeful.

Later, as we overlook the steep citrus orchards, he grabs an amanatsu from a nearby tree, a citrus fruit that looks like someone smashed an orange, and as we eat its juicy flesh, he tells me that it is hard to sell fruit that is not perfectly round and tied up in a ribbon. To come up with a plan to use the tons of crop, they reached out to winemaker Hirotake Ooka and asked him if he might be able to ferment citrus as he does grapes. Ooka, who after more than twenty years in France has returned to his homeland to make wine in Okayama, is a fervent supporter of the method taught by Fukuoka and agreed to try. "And so," Ooka tells us when we go see him in his home about two hours away, "one day enormous crates of citrus fruit showed up on my doorstep. I had no clue how to go about it, but now a few years later, what I do is simply throw the fruit, skin and all, in my old press and squash it slowly to release the juice and let it ferment on its own." The project is perfect for Ooka, since the cycle of citrus harvest is exactly opposite of grapes, giving the otherwise resting press (and its owner) something different to do in late winter.

LOCATION TIPS

SANZE NATURAL WINE BAR
Run by the quiet Takuro Shimizu (formerly from the Tokyo scene) who knows his stuff.

DOGO ONSEN
Attached to Matsuyama is one of the country's most famous onsen. Loved by emperors and depicted in *Spirited Away*, this bathhouse is being renovated yet remains accessible. Be warned: beautiful as the space may be, the water is murder-hot. After 15 minutes in 46-degree Celcius water I sprinted out and still red like a lobster, drank an iced beer in a nearby joint. Potentially the best beer I ever drank.

PAIRING ON THE MENU

The result is a bright yellow, low-alcohol slightly fizzy drink with a small amount of residual sugar and a pleasant zing, served with yuzu sorbet and a small strawberry and amanatsu mochi.

| WORDS | MASANOBU EGAMI | PHOTOS | AVA MEES LIST, HEAD SOMMELIER |

A pioneer and champion of the natural wine movement in Japan, Masanobu Egami, owner of Ethelvine in Kyoto, toasts the winemakers and their wines, and generations of growers.

Nippon Natural Wine Culture

IT WAS SOME 24 years ago that I first encountered what is called natural wine. I had already been involved in wine sales, but I became obsessed with the life in the wine that brought me emotions I had never experienced before. Philippe Jambon, Angiolino Maule, Alain Castex—at that time, their wines thrilled me.

Enthusiasts in Japan were among the first to import the European natural wine growers who had not yet gained a solid reputation in the world. It is thanks to them that the natural wine culture in Japan blossomed ahead of the rest of the world. The French natural wines introduced to Japan by Yoshio Ito, Yasuko Goda, and Junko Arai were sensational. I was also completely enamored by the wines brought to Japan from Italy by Hisato Ota. After I experienced these wines in Tokyo and Osaka, I started Ethelvine with the idea to educate people about natural wine in Kyoto, which was still an undeveloped area. It was difficult to gain a following, but we were blessed with friends and customers from restaurants of the same generation, and I believe that by now the culture has steadily taken root in Kyoto. If we call those predecessors who imported the wines the first generation, then we are the second generation, and I feel that a third generation of younger people is now taking up the baton. The culture is growing in its own unique way, sometimes mixing with and sometimes competing with the local climate in every corner of the country.

Having been exposed to the natural wine scene for more than 20 years, I have seen many changes. For example, the term orange wine, which is now commonly used, did not exist back in the day. It is not that such wines did not exist, but at that time they were part of the white wine category. I still sometimes struggle to specifically define orange wine to my customers and I continue to stubbornly say white wine. Another example is that I notice these days more and more wine is made from grapes that have not reached the ripeness that they should have. A balance between acidity and ripeness is the real appeal of wine, but I feel that the ratio of acidity versus ripeness is becoming stronger. Some of the reasons for the changes may be the influence of the market on winemaking as well as climate change in recent years. At Ethelvine we would like to continue to strive as one of the cavistes in Kyoto with our own views. I believe that the individuality of terroir, vintages and varietals can only be expressed when wines are at least moderately ripe.

WHAT ABOUT winemaking in Japan? The country has a wide range of climates, from Hokkaido in the north to Kyushu and Okinawa in the south. The fact that the history of winemaking in Japan is still young compared to Europe is due in part to the difficulty of growing *Vitis vinifera* in its mostly hot and humid climate. For the size of the country, there are not many areas where it is possible to take on this challenge and even more so when it comes to biodynamic viticulture. It is limited to a few places and even so it requires the unrelenting efforts of producers in their vineyards. However, the quality of some Japanese natural wine growers over the past few years has been remarkable, and the number of new farmers who are taking on winemaking is increasing. Bruce Gutlove and his wife Ryoko, who run 10R winery in Iwamizawa, Hokkaido, play a big part in this. In addition to vinifying their own grapes, they also provide a winery and facilities to grape growers who do not have their own space and generously share their skills with them. They have nurtured a number of producers who have gone on to become successful winemakers on their own. One is Takahiko Soga of Domaine Takahiko, also located in Yoichi, Hokkaido. Those who have trained under him also continue to produce unique and wonderful wines. Eishi Okamoto is a lone and honorable winemaker in Hokuto, in the Yamanashi Prefecture. Rather than learning from European winemaking methods, he faces the climate and soil and listens to their voices. He continues to nurture Japanese wines that coexist with both harshness and serenity.

We are convinced that their wines, which express the unique geological, climatic, and microbiological environment of Japan, are worthy of being recognized around the world. Even though it will be a difficult road ahead, I have high hopes for the future of these new wine growers who have chosen to take on this new challenge.

Having had the opportunity to work with noma in Kyoto, I feel as though I was able to experience Japanese products in a new and deeper way. I learned a great deal from their positive and humble attitude toward Japanese and Kyoto culture. The energy they brought to our team and their Japanese colleagues through their deep spirit of exploration and action is immeasurable. I look forward to seeing the team members again.

WORDS   CAROLYNE LANE, HEAD OF TEA AND COFFEE

SERVING TEA IN JAPAN

Delivering an honest tea program involved working with like-minded people who respect tradition but whose deep knowledge allows them to make their own rules.

PHOTO: CAROLYNE LANE

NOMA IN KYOTO

TOKUYA meets us on a hillside just outside the small village of Kamo. He's wearing a t-shirt bearing the slogan "CHATSUMI GIRL IS FANTASY." He later explains the slogan's significance: in pre-industrialized Japanese tea farming, the processing of tea was hard labor that required physical strength. Because of this, women (or chatsumi girls) picked tea leaf in the field and men handled the more physical task of processing it. These were both forms of skilled work which were common in Japanese society. However, as Japanese agriculture became increasingly mechanized, people began to lose touch with their tea farming traditions. The image of the chatsumi girl, delicately picking leaf in the field became nothing more than a marketing tool. But, Tokuya continues, this is an image that no longer reflects reality.

An eighth-generation tea farmer, he almost lost his life to "style over substance" agriculture. This tendency stretches beyond the chatsumi girl to include the heavy use of pesticides and fertilizers used to achieve a certain aesthetic, both in the field and in the leaf. Japanese sencha attains its green color and characteristic umami flavor with greater ease by way of this intervention. It was after years of exposure to the chemicals involved in his family's sencha farm that Tokuya got sick. The subsequent exploration of organic farming practices was his way of healing, both his own body and the land on which he would come to raise his two children.

"How does my field look, compared to others you've visited?" He asks this almost contemptuously; he knows that they are worlds apart. One can barely see the tea trees beneath a thick layer of vines and wild grasses. You would be forgiven for assuming that the field were neglected or abandoned. He appears proud of this, keen to demonstrate the virtues of this untamed system.

"The earth knows already what it needs. The weeds that are growing here are the food the soil has decided it needs. So, I let them grow to full maturity before I weed them out."

"The earth knows already what it needs. The weeds that are growing here are the food the soil has decided it needs. So, I let them grow to full maturity before I weed them out. Once picked, this vegetation is left to rot where the weeds once stood. In this way, the soil receives exactly the nourishment it has already decided it needed."

All this weeding is done by hand—one hand—Tokuya's. When asked why he doesn't arrange help for this incredibly labor intensive, four-month-long task, he explains: "It is almost impossible to teach someone what should be weeded and what should be left. This took me decades to learn."

Ferns for example, are allowed to grow in certain areas uninterrupted. Their root systems help to stabilize the soil in places where erosion causes entire fields to slide downhill. A kind of natural protection against a pervasive problem in this extreme landscape, with its severe slopes. One such example appears as a dense, vertical wall of green. Zairai, a native tea variety, is growing here reinforced by a whole host of other kinds of vegetation. This, on one side; on the other, a bamboo forest sloping downhill. The trees appear to be felled in a kind of formation. Tokuya explains that each year, he cuts down a specific constellation of trees, depending on how the zairai is growing. This promotes air flow to the field. As bamboo grows quickly, invasively even, this is a job that must be tended to regularly. He seems excited that the topic of airflow has entered the conversation and goes on to explain that the space left by removing matured weeds and grasses also creates room for increased airflow between the tea trees, eliminating the need for the motor-driven fans that line most Japanese tea fields.

FOR THE PAST 20 years, noma has worked with people who operate in the same spirit as Tokuya. Those who delight in and work with the natural world. From the forager engaged in a constant exploration of wild flavors, to the asparagus farmer who is quite literally obsessed with growing asparagus. These are individuals who don't necessarily follow the "rules" of their chosen fields. Working this way is rare, requiring a deep understanding of the craft, and this comes with

1. Tokuya stands in a field of Zairai, a native Kyoto tea cultivar.
2. Dense ferns engulf the Zairai tea trees.
3. In conversation with Tokuya in his Ryori room.

time. Experience has afforded Tokuya the intuition to understand what his trees need to grow healthily and the sensitivity to read microscopic signs from the landscape around him. It also lends him the confidence to strategically break the rules of tea farming where appropriate. Indeed, he has made mistakes. One can't really observe the effect of a change in farming practices for at least a year or more. Tea farming operates on a different time scale to, say, vegetable farming and the trace of the human hand takes longer to materialize. Having recognized this, and wanting a place to test farming methodology, Tokuya began keeping a hobby vegetable garden alongside his farm. Here, he is free to play, to experiment and farming methods are trialed on peppers or eggplants before being employed to care for his precious tea trees.

Later, he takes us to his dojo, located between sloping tea fields, in a house built by a member of his grandfather's generation. These frame houses have become a rarity, so few nowadays retain the knowledge to safely erect such a structure made of uneven, misshapen timbers. Here, Tokuya teaches aikido and mixed martial arts to members of the local community. He is keen to illustrate how his martial arts practice informs his farming. And so he invites us to try a handful of exercises.

The first involves striking a punching bag held by a partner. He demonstrates that the perceived weight of the punch increases by letting go of all unnecessary tension. The muscles of the arm remain completely limp right up until the moment of impact. "Tea farming is the same," he explains. "It's important to let go of all unnecessary tension. I don't weed the field until right before harvest. In other words, the fist is not clenched until it has to be."

He encourages us to simplify our movements: the drawing back of a fist and swinging of an arm are eliminated in favor of a more simple forward motion. This small change in

perspective charged a gesture with enough power to knock a man off his feet. The idea is not to employ as much force as possible, but to work with the natural balance of the body to achieve the desired outcome. It's this awareness, a kind of bodily intuition, which he brings to his tree trees.

There is power in restraint. These trees are not forced into producing desired outcomes; rather, gently with as little force as possible. In such a dynamic, where the interventions to the trees external environment are minimal, the tree's core is free to reserve the energy to become strong, much like the hand that farms it. The result is tea that is distinct in flavor: Tokuya jokes about his black tea tasting smoky, almost like whisky. This we blended with hojicha, a kind of Japanese roasted tea, for our juice and tea pairing. His beautifully floral white tea became a best seller on our after-dinner selection.

WHEN building a tea program for a pop-up in Japan, a country so steeped in tea culture, we had to make some carefully considered decisions. With this culture comes a set of expectations and rules. It was deeply important to us not to misrepresent any aspects of Japanese tea culture. That said, it was equally important to work in a way that felt authentic to us, with the kinds of producers that we feel excited by. So when faced with the question of tea ware, we opted not to use anything with cultural significance, despite the plethora of perfectly beautiful options available to us. Instead, we designed and had made a set of teapots specifically for our tea service. These were simple, balloon-like shapes made of glass. The tea and its color were clearly visible. In essence, it was the tea itself, and not the culture surrounding it that we wanted placed center stage. This freed us to make some exciting sourcing decisions.

One such example comes from a farmer 30-minutes east of Tokuya's farm called Kenichi. Unlike Tokuya, Kenichi does not come from a tea-producing family. He bought his farm, spread across a high-elevation slope in Nara some 20 years ago and set about the task of learning everything he could about tea farming. This exploration led him to reach out to previous generations of farmers, elders whose techniques predate the industrialized practices which dominate the agricultural landscape today. From there, he travelled abroad to learn more tea farming techniques from other countries. In his own words: "Today I am a Japanese sencha farmer. Tomorrow I could be a Chinese white tea farmer. Perhaps tomorrow I am making Taiwanese oolong."

His spirit of exploration and creativity has yielded some unexpected and exciting results, such as the first offering on our juice and tea pairing. It was an infusion of every part of the tea tree: stem, leaf and flower. The inclusion of tea flower is unusual. Most farmers remove the flowers of the plant to redirect nutrients to the leaves. Kenichi spent some time exploring how the aroma of the flower might be captured in an infusion. He noticed that simply infusing the flowers themselves didn't work; the resulting brew was weak and uninspiring. And then he remembered jasmine tea.

In high-grade jasmine tea, jasmine flowers are spread among the tea leaves as they dry. Each day they are removed and replaced with fresh flowers. Their scent is trapped in the leaf to give it its characteristic floral aroma. After employing the same technique, Kenichi was finally able to capture the aroma of his tea flowers. We blended this scented black tea with sannenbancha, or, tea made from the plant's stem. Kenichi's sannenbancha is made from younger, tender stem, all the way to full-on chunks of tea branch. Its flavor lies somewhere in between vanilla and cedarwood. The conversation between it and the flower tea was something special. Never before had we been able to taste the entire tea tree in one cup.

The craft that made this tea possible was a perfect demonstration of what we wanted to achieve with the tea program as a whole; to find new expressions for Japanese tea, while respecting traditions that came before.

EVERY ingredient at noma carries a story. We chose to expand upon two here but could have told a number of others. How many restaurants can say that they had a black tea laboriously hand-picked and made just for their guests? We are enormously grateful to Fumiaki and Doumen of the Tsukigase tea garden for this.

And then there is Yuko, of the Mitosaya Botanical Distillery, with whom we enjoyed a spirited herbal tea collaboration. To this day we exchange stories, herbal blends and production methods with one another. We continue to be inspired by the people we worked with, and that inspiration continues to find new forms. In this way, the ripple effects of the Kyoto pop-up have followed us, all the way back home to Copenhagen.

> The craft that made this tea possible was a perfect demonstration of what we wanted to achieve with the tea program as a whole; to find new expressions for Japanese tea, while respecting traditions that came before.

1

2

3

4

PHOTOS: FRITZ BUZIEK

100

1. Sannenbancha

Sannenbancha, a tea made from tea branch, farmed by Kenichi.

2. Sakura leaf

A collaboration between myself and Yuko from the Mitosaya botanical garden. Oxidised and fermented sakura leaves, made in a similar style to black tea.

3. Hojicha and Kōcha

A blend of hojicha, a roasted late harvest tea from the Tsukigase estate, blended with kōcha (black tea) from Tokuya Yamazaki.

4. Chiran Sencha

Sencha from Kagoshima, organically farmed by Chiran Nōen under the guidance of the Nuruki sisters. Part of our tea and juice pairing.

Special Harvest and Blossom

A sparkling infusion of Sakura blossom and a specially harvested black tea from the Tsukigase Estate.

Tripping for Tea

A cup of tea at Noma Kyoto had to reflect the values of the restaurant. This meant visiting tea makers to better understand the process of tea farming so we could make informed sourcing decisions. Along the way we met some deeply passionate growers, who carved their own path in an otherwise strict tradition of tea making in Japan. Their commitment to biodiversity and daring in trying different farming and processing methods yielded teas that were highly expressive and singular, perfect pairings for our menu. A special thanks to our friends at Io Teahouse in Copenhagen. Many of the relationships we built would not have been possible without your support.

PHOTOS: CAROLYNE LANE

1. Tokuya brewing black tea out of the back of his pickup truck.

2. Our Beverage Director, Mees, and Tokuya-san inspecting the soil around his Yabukita trees.

3. Tokuya-san demonstrating how Aikido informs his farming practice.

4. Sifting matcha.

5. Tea trees shaded by wild ferns.

6. Kenichi-san and Carolyne taste some tea in the tea field.

7. Our barista, Tsubasa in the tea field.

6

7

8

9

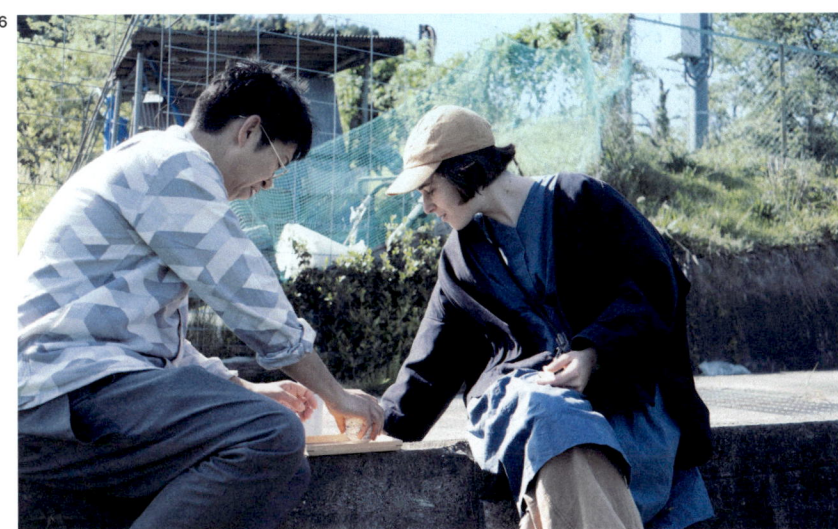

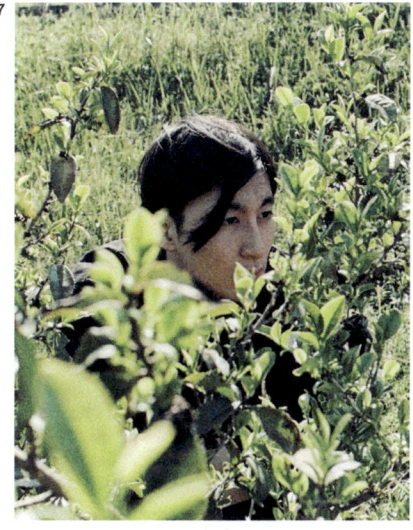

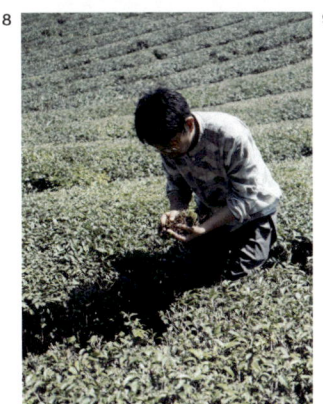

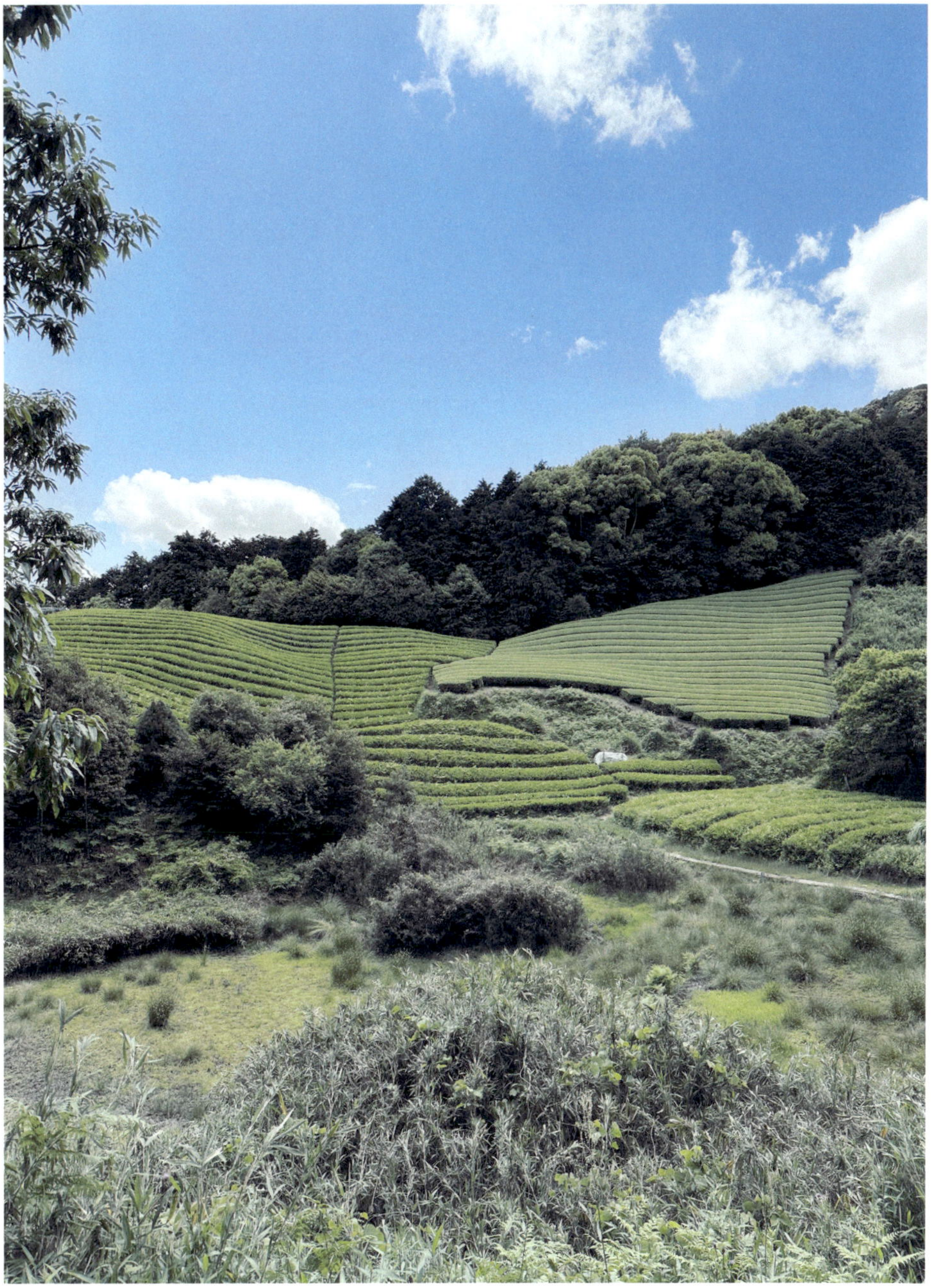

8. Kenichi demonstrates the health of his soil.

9. Tokuya's wild tea fields next to the carefully manicured ones of his father.

10. The noma front of house team visits Tokuya at his farm—somehow all 16 of us survived the ride to the tea field in the back of his truck.

10

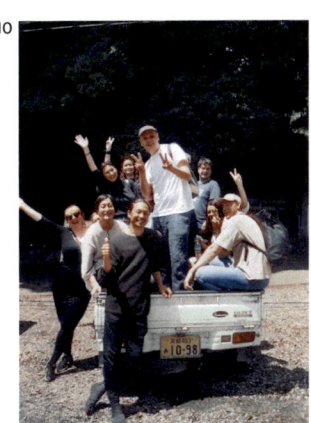

A letter for Noma in Kyoto

Dear Everybody at noma,

About that time when everything, including the mountains and seas, sang songs of a pale pink spring.

I'm still living in the continuation of that dream I had (at Noma Kyoto).

A journey of life that began from the deep forest of Denmark, and I was invited to the forest of the sea (the dining room at Ace) nurtured by the forest of the land.

I slipped back to memories of my childhood, when I used to pick pebbles on the beach and walked along the seashore to a garden of joy.

Denmark, Japan, and all the land in between are intertwined within this forest called Earth. I truly sensed that their plants and creatures were also connected, sharing inspiration amongst each other.

We are deeply grateful that our tea resonated with the beautiful harmony you created at Noma Kyoto.

A toast to the future, and everything it will bring.

Kenichi Igawa,
KENICHI HEALTH FARM

March 21, 2023

WORDS   RISA KAMIO   STYLING   CHRISTINE RUDOLPH   PHOTOGRAPHY   DITTE ISAGER

ART OF THE TABLE

The Scandi-Japan blend extended from the menu to the tablewares of Noma Kyoto with plates, bowls and sake cups sourced from the potters and artisans of Japan.

NOMA IN KYOTO

Earthy, close to nature, quirky, personality: key words and ideas drove the Japan-wide search for artisans and the products that could furnish the tables for Noma Kyoto. Along with ceramicists were suppliers of hand-dyed hemp and linen, glass and cutlery.

JUST AS the kitchen and beverage teams searched Japan for ingredients, produce, wine and sake, noma's in-house interior stylist Christine Rudolph and I had the exciting task of sourcing materials for tableware and decor. Apart from exploring the enormous discipline of ceramics, we investigated bamboo, glass, wood, lacquerware, plant weavings, hand-dyed hemp, linen, hand-forged iron knives and rattan, as well as seaweed and leaves.

Starting in the second half of 2021, Christine and I made moodboards developed from close conversations with René, who wanted to use this collection back in Copenhagen after the pop-up. Key words and concepts were earthy, close relation to nature, personality, quirky.

Japan has a history of pottery that extends over 10,000 years and is deeply infused within Japanese culture. From its earliest forms as earthenware from Okinawa, it evolved as techniques were introduced from Korea and China, and amid later prosperity the tea ceremony influenced its development of unique Japanese cultural characteristics.

Important historical areas of pottery production are scattered all over Japan and potters in countless places throughout the country developed their unique designs, methods and traditions.

> Since ancient times, the Japanese have appreciated and found beauty in imperfection or being ambiguous. People tended to accept and appreciate transition or destruction of things as part of its nature.

At the beginning of 2022, we delved into this vast universe of Japanese pottery, the diverse world of artists and artisans. We worked online most of the time and when travel was permitted, we visited a few artisans whom we had already started to work with. We saw hand-built wood-fired kilns, handled different kinds of clay, saw glazing techniques and the materials that composed the glazes. When choosing the Japanese makers, it was important that the pieces had some kind of earthy and interesting character that also paid tribute to all the Japanese traditions handed down over generations. At first, we looked for artists in the Kyoto area, but we discovered ceramicist located all over Japan. While Japanese craft was the main focus, at the same time we wanted the mix of Scandinavian aesthetics to show through in the tableware. So we added pieces from some of our favorite makers in Denmark..

Selecting the plates was the top priority but this large-scale project also included the creation of a restaurant space and the myriad tasks before the arrival of staff to Japan.

Christine and I sent images of potential makers to each other regardless of the time, early in the morning and late at night. We had a long list of people we wanted to work with, and the biggest job was to edit this down. We chose about 50 artisans whose style worked within the brief, and we ended up working with 21 Japanese and 9 Danish artists.

Communications with all the artisans was a great adventure for me and involved paying attention to every detail. Since ancient times, the Japanese have appreciated and found beauty in imperfection or being ambiguous. People tended to accept and appreciate transition or destruction of things as part of their nature, and therefore the process itself and the behaviors in the process were important; sometimes even more important than the outcome.

All these have helped to develop the culture of omotenashi. This is also reflected in the way the artists work and in the work itself. It reflects where they live, the kind of clay and water they can source, the kind of glazing and firing they work with, and everything in between. Therefore I found it was important to approach and communicate with great care, talking to the artists directly, rather than only exchanging short messages. Enclosing a letter or a simple card when sending samples back was another way to show sincerity, even though it may have seemed like doing too much inefficient work for my non-Japanese colleagues.

Proper behavior, craftmanship, manners and procedures are all involved in the concept of beauty. Consider this story of failure. I had help from the team with packing the samples to return. Japan is famous for its packaging methods, and the standard of wrapping skills is high, because of its long and rich history of packing and wrapping. I gave only the guideline to "wrap it so that it does not break". The team packed it relatively freely and as a result, I received negative feedback and lost trust. It's not a matter of not breaking, it's a matter of how you wrap. The way you wrap shows your personality. For Japanese, to wrap is not only something functional, but it entails a kind of invisible message. Embarrassingly, I was too busy and exhausted to pay attention to that. The culture of wrapping in Japan has been passed down for thousands of years, and the definition of the verb "to wrap" has several layers. Wrapping exists not only for functionality or beauty, but has evolved over time to encompass practicality, beauty, artistry and even faith. Wrapping gifts with a piece of paper has its origins in religious ceremonies, and while this tradition has changed over time its inspiration can still be seen. Wrapping with fabric and the use of particular envelopes have their own origins and traditions. Wrapping has been a way to communicate, to convey seasonality, courtesy, and to send the message that the receiver is important to the sender. The Japanese symbol "to wrap" has its origin in the picture of a fetus growing inside a mother, indicating that "to wrap" involves not only the practical aspect of carrying, but protecting something that you gift to loved ones.

IN FEBRUARY 2022, the first ceramic samples arrived. We organized three big sample meetings with more than 150 pieces and some vintage items in Kyoto and Copenhagen, and also had countless conversations with René and the team.

After these meetings, we had a clearer idea of where we wanted to go and the research trips began. We couldn't visit all the makers but meeting even a few and seeing the amazing hand-built wood-fired kilns gave us a better understanding of how the Japanese potters worked.

In Nara we drove through lush forest to a tranquil farmhouse and were greeted by the artisan. In the garden we saw his kiln under a simple roof construction, with ceramics scattered everywhere, mistakes though they looked perfect to us, broken pieces, others waiting to be fired in the kiln. Your eyes didn't know where to rest. (A giant leaf from a huge magnolia lay among a pile of clay, its size and texture mesmerizing. This leaf ended up on the first course tray—but that is another story for another day.) We entered the beautiful studio, dust and stacks of ceramic pieces everywhere. He took us through the building, up an alley where he displayed some larger pieces, the textured clay walls the most beautiful backdrop, like a gallery. He produced sake cup for us and some of his larger items were used as decoration at the restaurant.

Even after figuring out who to work with, there were challenges. One of them was timing, which was very tight. Potters using natural kilns don't fire very often and they have firm schedules that involve agreements with the local area about when and how often they fire because of smoke. Quantity was another challenge as we required many plates, but these artisans usually produced small numbers.

All this involved countless video calls and messages with every single ceramicist and artisan, adjusting sizes, shapes and glaze, to follow the requirements of the test kitchen, as the menu development was in progress while we finalized the order.

Because of the limited time frame, we chose from existing designs by the makers, and this allowed the uniqueness of each artist to stand out and any adjustments respected their original design. It was quite magical seeing it all come together, somehow with a connection across the entire collection. The pieces from Denmark and elsewhere somehow had a link to the Japanese pottery—perhaps because of the materials used in the glaze, the wood-firing or the muted tones—while some of the Japanese items had a Scandinavian appearance. All harmonized on the table, the works from all the different artists becoming the tableware collection for Noma Kyoto, a palette of muted earth colors combined with the splashes of red lacquerware.

Each piece embodied the creator; the work, professionalism and identity of each artisan, all heading in the same direction, somehow overlapped. Each one loves their profession and the materials they work with. They have passion, similar to the noma team who love cooking and making people happy. Although expressed in different ways, there is an underlying shared philosophy between the artisans and we who work in hospitality, both creating things that can only be made by the time and place and the people themselves.

It was quite magical seeing it all come together. All harmonized on the table, the works of all the artists, a palette of muted earth colors combined with the splashes of red lacquerware.

It was important that the chosen pieces had the character of Japanese tradition blended with the noma aesthetic.

KINTSUGI

A term now universally known, kintsugi is the repair technique of ceramic and porcelain tableware that is often served as a metaphor for life. A process that gives way to a landscape that is possible only after breakage. What is broken is not discarded but respectfully and carefully put back together. The Japanese understanding of wabi-sabi is at the heart of kintsugi: embracing transience and impermanence and finding beauty in the natural cycle of the universe. Damaged pieces are repaired with the use of urushi tree sap, blended with other natural materials based on the type of fracture. A decorative touch of gold is applied at the very end, further highlighting the unique story of each piece. The repair requires the curing of urushi with each step, and thus the entire process takes at minimum two - three months start to finish. But we are left with a beautifully repaired piece of tableware that is absolutely food safe and incredibly durable. Without kintsugi, we might end up throwing away so much more than necessary. And so, during our stay in Kyoto, some of us attended workshops at POJ Studio to learn this traditional Japanese technique. It enabled us to embrace flaws and find calm in repairing each piece little by little, bit by bit.

Deep gratitude to all the craftspeople and our kintsugi teachers. Countless arigato to them!

The Makers

1. Tetsuya Kobayashi
2. Aya and Kazuhiro Tsubota
3. Jackie Iwami
4. Yoshihiro Funaki
5. Hannah Blackall-Smith
6. Tomomi Kawakami
7. Ann-Charlotte Ohlsson
8. Kaori Uchida
9. Anne Mette Hjortshøj
10. Kristine Vedel Adeltoft
11. Keiko Murakami
12. Roberto Jun Yuasa
13. Tomomi Mizutani
14. Atsushi Ogata
15. Masaichi Ishida
16. Mai Hvid Jørgensen
17. Noritaka Yamamoto
18. Nobue Ibaraki
19. Yoshiaki Tadaki
20. Tokuhito Marukawa
21. Tenshin Juba
22. Kei Condo
23. Toru Hatta
24. Asuka Juba
25. Janaki Larsen
26. Saya Okihara
27. Nobuhiko Tanaka

1

2

3

4

5

6

7

8

9

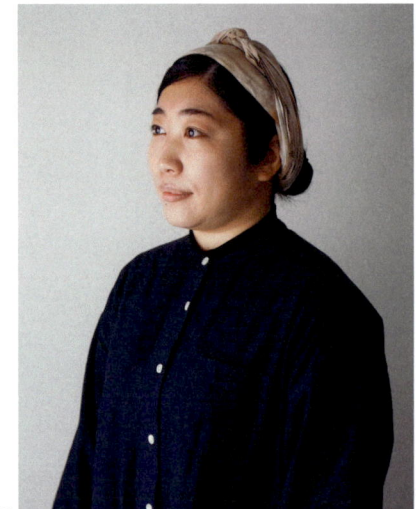

10

11

12

114

WORDS   CHRISTINE RUDOLPH, NOMA RESIDENT STYLIST

Hidden Treasures

For Noma Kyoto the decoration had to feel beautiful, special and curated, but not like a gallery. Finds from the city's flea markets ended up as a big part of the decor.

HUNTING FOR TREASURES in flea markets is like hunting for mushrooms. You must have patience, linger, let the environment hit you and then suddenly you see. The first one is the hardest. Maybe at first you don't see anything, but after a while, treasure after treasure.

You can find the unexpected, like the most perfectly shaped dried mushroom that ended up on display in the principal dining room; it was kind of cut in half and it looked like it was growing out of the wall. These kinds of pieces you can't plan for, but often they are there if you look hard enough. I very much follow intuition when I go to flea markets, have an open mind and let the feet and eyes direct me. I don't recommend going in a big group, though that can be fun, but being in your zone is important.

These decorations were to be added to the interior design of OEO Studio, with whom we had been intensely collaborating in the year leading up to the pop-up, so I had a clear idea of the textures and style that we were to source for the space, and for final touches and ambiance we aimed for.

I clearly remember the first morning we went, Risa and I, on the first research trip in April 2022, still under lockdown and we entered Japan on a working visa. We entered through the huge gate to the temple grounds. On the very first table on the right, were dried persimmons. Risa bought some and the taste of these will stay with me forever. On the next table, the tiniest bonsai trees, and suddenly I wanted to buy them all. This was going to be a very special morning.

We walked through food stands and reached a small side street and a display of natural string and fabric all neatly laid out in baskets. We bought samples: string that was thin pieces of bark, others of hemp, and flax, some linen fabric in the most beautiful colors. I was not exactly sure what use

Christine and Risa exploring one of the many flea markets of Kyoto.

these items would be, but the fabric ended up being part of our ceiling display in the two smaller dining rooms. We later discovered that this was a company called Aoni Textiles and we visited their amazing warehouse-like studio where there was so much inspirational knowledge and an overwhelming display of fabric made of natural fibers.

We continued our hunt among vendors of ceramics and fabric, and found tiny sake cups, no single one alike. That started the idea of the noma sake cup collection, great fun to collect over time. We had the sake cups for serving, so these were just for display.

Suddenly we saw knives, all kitchen knives, with an amazing handle of bamboo, done in a very special way with a thin string of bamboo neatly wrapped in a crisscross pattern and then lacquered. They felt so natural and special, not too refined like some lacquer we came across. Risa spoke to the knife maker, yes she was very much the person to be with; interaction would be impossible without a Japanese speaker. We were excited, if we could adjust these a bit, this would be a real find! This was the start of a very inspiring and educational relationship. We later went to Yoshihiro Funaki's workshop in the mountains on the outskirt of Kyoto, a small wooden shed where he made these beautiful knives, all hand-forged and every handle made by him. These knives became a very big part of the utensils that guests used dining at the restaurant.

That morning became one of many, I didn't count all the trips to the flea markets but we went many, many times. By the time of the last trip to Kyoto to set up the restaurant, my assistant Sarah and I had become experts, splitting up, walking fast through all the lanes to see if anything special was there. Sometimes we needed a lot of a single item, so you needed to be early to get the whole load. Afterwards, we would walk the whole market again slowly and with a more open mind, a good tactic if you have special items you are looking for.

We learned about ceramics and fabric, met vendors who would bring new items for us the following market day. We found sticks, odd pieces of tree trunk, dried leaves, half-made baskets and old koji and tofu trays that ended up being storage and display for the handmade knives and other flatware used daily at the restaurant. The crazy beautiful woodwork craftsmanship of these trays would make an established carpenter in Denmark envious. We found large moon jars, artwork, pottery, lacquer-ware; we learned about the history and the use of items about which we had no idea. We dragged bags and boxes. I don't think people really think about the physical toll to go through these huge grounds, but so totally worth it.

So yes, Kyoto flea markets became a very big part of Noma Kyoto decor. Not the whole part; we had our favorite artist making special pieces, we had plants, greenery, seaweed and flowers. But somehow those unknown, hidden treasure, one-of-a-kind pieces, really made a big impact.

Cultural Infusion

How to translate the physical presence and essence of noma in Copenhagen to noma in Kyoto? Just as the kitchen worked with culinary masters, the space required master craft workers to provide authenticity with a twist.

Borrowed landscape: the dining room, a double-height space on the third floor of a 1926 building renovated by Kengo Kuma, overlooked a garden and was transformed by the noma team.

BASED IN a 1926 building by modernist architect Tetsuro Yoshida, the Ace Hotel Kyoto was renovated by Kengo Kuma and Associates, excellent credentials for the location of Noma Kyoto. But how to transform the third-floor, double-height space overlooking a rooftop garden into a dining space that resonated with noma and its culinary vision for Kyoto?

Just as the noma culinary style employed fresh local ingredients, the physical dining experience blended Nordic and Japanese culture with the use of local materials and traditional craftsmanship.

Copenhagen-based interior designers OEO Studio also had a project office in central Tokyo and worked closely with the noma team and especially with noma's resident stylist Christine Rudolph. Combining the similarities and intrinsic differences between Japanese and Scandinavian culture infused Noma Kyoto with the strong design traditions of both to create an atmosphere of warm, handmade tactility and dimmed lighting. With a welcoming yet surprising use of materials and employing an earthy palette, the interiors paid tribute to the wider cultural context and offered a once-in-a-lifetime experience. Transforming a space can be a challenging task, yet it is also an extremely rewarding experience when everything comes together in perfect synchrony.

The key inspiration for Noma Kyoto was Japanese culture and Kyoto. The interior is an accolade of the richness in craftsmanship, tradition and cultural heritage. In the spirit of Kyoto's rich craft heritage, the interior design was achieved by collaborating with some of the best local craftspeople working with traditional materials such as ceramics, tatami, textile, bamboo and wood. The team's passionate curiosity investigated working with materials in new and unexpected ways, such as using coloured tatami mats as acoustic wall screens and room dividers. For centuries, tatami mats were used as floor mats only but intrigued by the grassy aromas and qualities of tatami, the team fashioned them as walls panels, room dividers and minimalist decorations. Traditionally, tatami is crafted in a natural grass colour; at Noma Kyoto they were a range of greys as well as hues of sage and coral.

Architectural bamboo structures were also suspended from the ceiling to subtly assist with the zoning of the spaces as well as for decoration and to create a more intimate atmosphere. Kelp and seaweed are fascinating, beautiful and edible materials that play a major part in Japanese cuisine and figured strongly in the noma menu. Natural seaweed, clam plasma, dried kelp and traditional dyed tenugui textiles created a poetic illusion of a kelp forest, floating above the heads of diners and drifting to the rhythm of water.

The mochi wine cooler was an example of the adaptation of a traditional utensil used for generations to make mochi rice cakes. The vision was to create an extra-tall centrepiece crafted the traditional way to be used as a cooler for wine and sake. This simple standalone piece was created by craftsman Shuji Nakagawa from an immense log of wood with its raw bark exposed. Gradually, he shaped and gently refined the log before finally carving the bowl, which was originally intended for rice but now held ice. The final touch was the hammering of copper plates into bowl shapes that were nailed onto the wood.

Traditional tenugui fabrics—common household cloths—were dyed and hung from the ceiling to evoke an underwater kelp forest floating above diners. Additional dried seaweeds, leaves, ceramics, and plants found homes in the unique space.

The key inspiration for Noma Kyoto was Japanese culture and Kyoto. The interior is an accolade of the richness in craftsmanship, tradition and cultural heritage.

Beyond the Veil

The inspiration for noren sprang from necessity but over centuries the role of the woven fabric dividers has transcended merely separating the outside from the inside into a transformative experience.

IN THE LIVELY streets of Kyoto, a constant sense of movement prevails. It's not just the hustle of people going about their day, the zigzag of bicycles through traffic, or even the nimble maneuvering of Toyota Crown Comfort taxis in narrow lanes. Even when the wind rests in Japan's ancient capital, there's one sentinel that remains ever-present and ever-moving: the noren.

These fabric dividers, which have graced doorways since the 700s, are more than mere curtains. They act as a gentle barrier between the present and what awaits beyond. While they might obscure a clear view, they don't mute the sizzling sound of skewered chicken caramelizing, the aromatic allure of freshly toasted tea leaves, or the tantalizing glimpse of a craftsman engrossed in his art. Passing through a noren is transformative; the bustling world fades away, leaving only a moment of discovery and intrigue, a moment one wishes could linger forever.

Like many historical inventions, the inspiration for noren sprang from necessity. They shielded homes from the elements—the sun, wind, and dust. Originally, their design was mostly utilitarian, simple fabric barriers fulfilling their protective role.

The term noren traces its roots back to the late 14th century, during the twilight of the Kamakura period. During the 13th and 14th centuries, merchants began to craft more detailed noren, utilizing these fabrics as advertising canvases for their trades. The color of a noren often hinted at the business it shielded: white, reminiscent of sugar, for confectionary shops; a brownish orange for tobacco sellers; and the indigo blue of aizome for restaurants, this traditional dye used for its insect-repelling properties. Legend has it that in the Edo Period (17th to mid-19th century), satisfied restaurant patrons would rub their hands on a noren upon departure as a gesture of appreciation for a delightful meal.

During the Edo Period, Japan closed its borders, which led to a surge in domestic manufacturing and elevated the stature of the merchant class. These merchants, in search of a striking means to showcase their goods, utilized norens amongst other means. These fabric dividers beautifully telegraphed the merchandise within. The Meiji Restoration (mid-19th to the early 20th century) led to an increased emphasis on education, which bolstered the literacy rate. Consequently, noren designs began to incorporate words and names, thereby diversifying their visual language.

Over the years, as the cultural importance of noren swelled, so too did the dedication to their artisanal craftsmanship. An increased focus on design found its way into the creation of norens.

The allure of the unknown, the tantalizing glimpse, is part of the mysterious charm of the noren.

Increasing literacy changed the nature of the noren as more explicit information could be conveyed.

Specific colours were used to identify the nature of businesses and sometimes kamon, or family crests, were incorporated into the curtains.

WORDS SAMIRO YUNOKI TRANSLATION RISA KAMIO

INSPIRED ENTRY

The design of the noren for Noma Kyoto originated from a creative process that started with the subconscious. The shapes and colors fell from the pen of Samiro Yunoki, the 101 year old master of stencil dyeing.

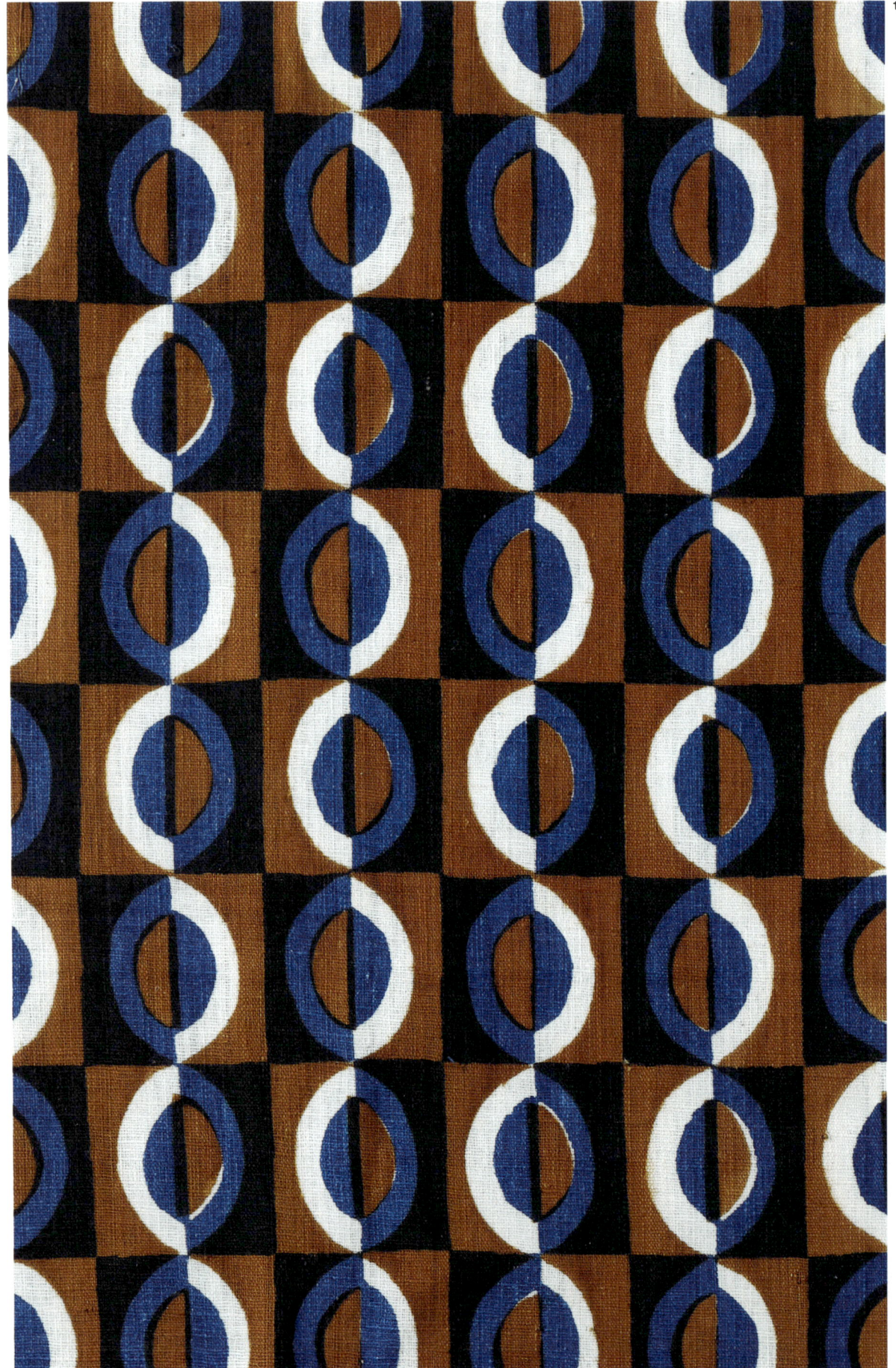

PONDERING the design of a new noren I always consider and prioritize these simple points: Does everyone feel comfortable? Can you see through the other side of the noren? Or is it more hidden?

The design for the Noma Kyoto noren is born from these thoughts. As I worked on it, I realized that I had made a mistake in the size of the design so the vertical lines on the top and bottom of the noren were a bit stretched. Even though I've done this for decades, mistakes can still happen, despite my experience, and I am humbled and glad that everyone was happy with the design.

When I create any sort of new design, the inspiration can come from different places—I don't have an exact way of working. Sometimes, designs will come to me naturally, out of my subconscious, and have no context with realistic objects, sights, or colors. Other times, I get inspiration from real sights and objects. In the case of the noren for Noma Kyoto, this design originated in the first instance from my creative process—my subconscious—and the shapes and colors naturally fell from my pen. The noma team did offer some inspirational materials, which provided a bit of context, but the completed design came about without overdoing it or overthinking it. It is always my wish for guests to feel relaxed in the restaurant, and my noren is the first thing that they see before they enter, so it can have a major impact on that.

I went on a trip to India many years ago, which was full of inspirational signs and objects that have since inspired my design. When I was there, I saw people eating with their hands in a cafeteria and many other everyday occurrences all of which inspired me: people sitting side-by-side in a bus; the shape of the carbon on the back of a copy slip and the roots and branches of an old tree in the park. I always take notes of what comes to my mind, and I never overlook any instance from where inspiration can come because inspiration is all around us, you just have to open your eyes.

1. Work of Samiro provided by the Japan Folk Art Museum. A design that led to Samiro's work on the noma noren.

2-3: Samiro working away in his studio.

"Even inconsequential objects have significance. There is no limit to the ways in which one could develop and refine that significance. For me, however, the beauty lies not in a deep reflection of the object, but rather in the uncritical, uncomplicated acceptance and appreciation of its natural state."

PHOTOS: TARO HIRANO

1. *Taskimon Pattern*, 1969. Considered one of his masterpieces, Samiro utilized various techniques to achieve this work—including scratching the 6 meter long paper with a tiny knife to yield a blurry outline and a unique chusen technique for stencil dyeing, which was revolutionary at the time.

2. Another chusen dyed cloth from the 1970s

3. *Circle*, 1969. This is a simple work made by dyeing the cloth with a single color of indigo, while keeping the white color of cotton itself in the background. Simple, but at the same time full of vitality with crescent-shaped thin patterns and irregularly arranged circles.

1. *Swallow1*, 2015. Samiro has created various iterations of swallows, which are an iconic subject for him.

2. *A, un*, unknown year of production. The translation of "A, un" can be understood as "ah, yeah" but it can also mean "being in a perfect rhythm" or "being able to understand each other's actions without having to say anything". Perhaps Samiro wanted to express this sentiment (or lack there of) with the two faces.

3. *Memory*, 2019.

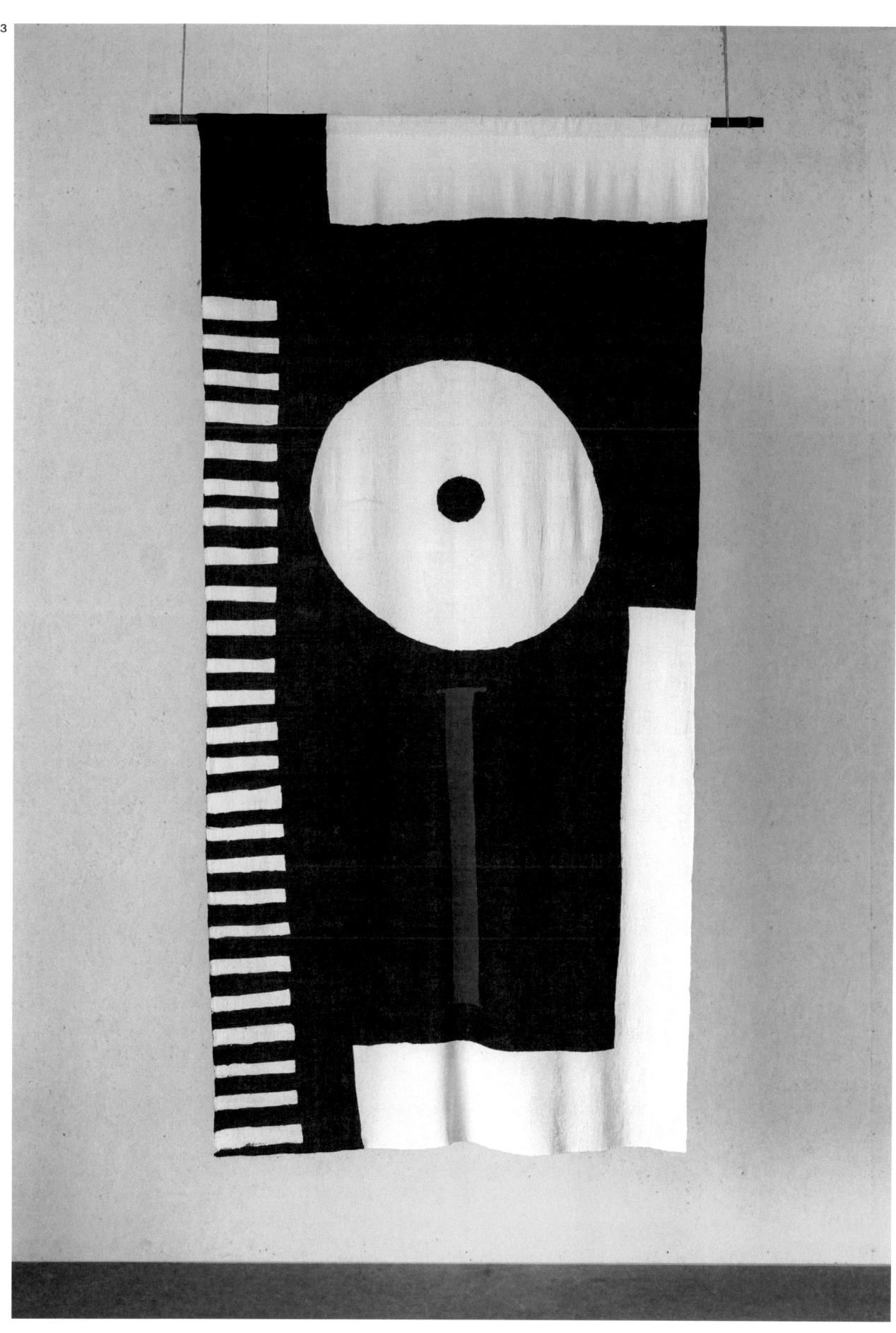

A cup of coffee in Japan awakens a complex cultural history, if you allow it. Weekenders Coffee Roastery dares to do just that.

Coffee

Ritual

A SEEMINGLY ENDLESS backdrop of scaffolding dwarfs a century-old mud-walled house. Within it is housed a little coffee shop. The only way to arrive at its doorstep is to cross a parking lot. As you approach, you might notice something rather curious. The space outside of a coffee shop is usually reserved for maximizing seating. Here though, these precious few square meters are ornamented by a carefully tended moss garden. Among the moss, a number of rope-tied stones (called sekimori-ishi) are placed in a way that makes it counter-intuitive to tread on these delicate plants. You cross the tiny garden and arrive at the counter marked by a slab of granite inset into the floor. Its size perfectly accommodates one person. Stand atop it, and only from here does the menu printed on fibrous washi paper come into view. To the right, bags of coffee are conspicuously placed to inform you of the cafe's current selection. To the left, a barista works calmly. They finish their task and walk the three steps to arrive parallel with you behind the counter. You may now place your order. There is no food offering, no noise to distract from what it is that you have come for: a cup of coffee. This is the Weekenders Tominokoji location. To look closely is to discover a plethora of subtle sensory delights that reflect the degree of sensitivity and care with which the owners Masahiro and Ayumi work.

THEIR ROASTERY is equally well-considered, serene and minimalist. The courtyard garden out the back is the perfect venue to drink a cup and enjoy a moment of contemplation in the dappled shade of its lone sakura tree. Curating these moments of introspection is a huge part of what Weekenders does. Over the years, they've become particularly concerned with exploring the relationship between coffee and Japanese culture.

Flicking through guidebooks of Japan, you are almost certain to encounter the imagery of a tea master, diligently bent over a matcha whisk, so iconic a part of Japanese culture is the tea ceremony. But tea is not the only beverage prepared with this degree of attention (although given its rich history, you'd be forgiven for thinking so).

Coffee's popularity in Japan was stunted by a ban on all imports following the Second World War. It wasn't until the early 60s that coffee became a readily available commodity. Its sudden introduction to the market brought with it some distinctly Japanese expressions of brewing coffee. The kissaten, a kind of traditional tea house, began to serve coffee that embodied a spirit of quality and craftsmanship. It was brewed slowly, in a pour-over style. Coffee brewing echoed the same ritualistic and mindful principles that we see in the tea ceremony, and yet despite their commonalities, these cultural points have never converged. Why? And what would a coffee ceremony look like? Weekenders began to ask these questions back in 2019. Since then, they have held seasonal coffee ceremonies in collaboration with Shiego Mashiro of Sfera design studio, who designed unique coffee brewing equipment and furniture specifically for this ceremonial context. In addition, they put a great deal of care into curating the interior spaces of each venue. These ceremonies have taken place in various locations, more recently taking place in Kyoto's historic Kosei-in temple. In conducting these ceremonies, Weekenders seek to create a moment of pause and reflection in the context of an industry that has developed at breakneck speed since its inception.

For many, coffee felt like a symbol of post-war American occupation, especially in subsequent years when the growth of the Japanese economy correlated with a rise in convenience culture. This included instant coffee and American-style commuter espresso bars. In many ways, Weekenders is a reaction to this rapid change in the coffee landscape. They strive to preserve that which is unique about drinking coffee in Japan, while uncovering new and meaningful relationships between it and the culture at large.

Whether you kneel on the tatami floor of Kosei-in, sit in the roastery garden, or lean against a parking lot bollard outside Tominokoji, there is a sense that you are drinking in much more than a cup of coffee. As you walk back across that parking lot, back into inner city Kyoto, it'll be hard not to be touched by this. Even if you lack the language to describe why, the experience of grabbing a cup of coffee, in all its mundane glory, will stay with you.

> They strive to preserve that which is unique about drinking coffee in Japan, while uncovering new and meaningful relationships between it and the culture at large.

Coffee ceremonies at the historic Kosei-in temple blend the rituals and mindfulness of the tea ceremony to introduce reflection and a sense of serenity that counters the caffeine-driven rush of convenience culture.

The calm of a classic Japanese interior: the ordered grid of tatami and shoji with a floor-level perspective, combined with nature and water induces internal quietude for the coffee ceremony.

WEEKENDERS TOMINOJOKI

Open every day except Wednesday, 7:30-18:00

WEEKENDERS COFFEE ROASTERY

Open Saturdays and Sundays, 10:00-17:00

Information on the coffee ceremonies can be found on the Weekenders website.

WORDS   ROBERT YELLIN, GALLERIST

Fired by Passion

The crafts of the kiln and the kitchen meet on the Japanese table. The long traditions of both reflect the unique qualities of seasonality and location.

"TO MAKE FOOD taste better put it in a better serving vessel," said the famed Japanese chef/artist Rosanjin Kitaōji (1883-1959), whom the Japanese revere to this day. Indeed the variety of tableware in Japan is unmatched and it's a joy to sit in a Japanese restaurant or home and have your senses as delighted by the table setting as the meal itself. These ceramics are the culmination of a craft that dates back millennia, the earliest pottery in Japan coming from the Jomon period (14000-300 BC). The firings in the neolithic period took place outdoors in bonfires, open pits, or ditches and temperatures were unlikely to exceed 700 degrees C, producing pieces that were quite fragile. The two styles associated with this early Japanese pottery are Jomon and Yayoi, and all were made without the potter's wheel and the kiln. Jomon has quite wild designs that even today resemble contemporary art, while Yayoi wares are calmer and symmetrical.

The introduction of Sueki ware to Japan from Korea in the middle of the 5th century marks a major turning point in Japanese ceramics, as both the anagama (single-chamber kiln) and the potter's wheel began to be used in Japan. Sueki was fired to 1,100-1,200 degrees C and generally made on the wheel. The grand traditions of Bizen ware, Shigaraki ware and Tamba ware—all listed among the Six Ancient Kilns—stem from the Sueki tradition, the wares named after the region where they were produced.

For many centuries the anagama kilns fired a wonderful creativity in Japanese aesthetics and ceramics, the unpredictability of the kiln, the flame, ash and minerals in the clay resulting in unique, earth-coloured pieces. In the early 17th century, the anagama lost its importance and was replaced by the noborigama multi-chamber climbing kilns that greatly improved productivity with up to twenty times more pots created in one firing. For glazed ware, such as Shino or Oribe, the noborigama brought a greater level of consistency and predictability to output, as well as economies of scale especially with the wood fuel. These days both the noborigama and anagama, which found a resurgence in the 1960s, are used by potters.

The products fired before kilns were introduced are generally referred to as earthenware and are characterized by low fire temperatures that make them porous and not so durable. The introduction of kilns created stoneware, which is water-proof and durable. Porcelain was introduced to Japan in the 17th century by Korean potters and started in Saga prefecture on the southern island of Kyushu. Clay that includes kaolin is fired at 1,200-1,400 degrees C, and the vitrification produces strong but delicate translucent wares that are much whiter than other forms of ceramics and take highly coloured glazes. Popular styles include Nabeshima, Kakiemon, Arita and Imari.

PHOTO: MITSURU WAKABAYASHI

The colors and textures of stoneware used in Japanese dining are the result of the unpredictability of kilns, minerals in clays and glazes and, of course, the hand of the maker.

Stoneware and porcelain, contemporary and antique, Japanese ceramics are displayed in the Robert Yellin Yakimono Gallery near the Philosopher's Path.

AS A YOUNG MAN in my twenties, I stayed at the lovely Arai ryokan in the Izu Peninsula. Our server brought all the dishes into my room and I was amazed and bewildered that just for me there were something like 20 dishes of various sizes and forms and not one matched the other. It was so very different from a western table and after that meal my entire dining aesthetic changed; I could never have a matching set of anything again.

The variety and diversity of pottery styles in Japan exceeds that of any country, each still has a place in Japanese culture today, used for tea, flowers and a meal. Seasonality plays a pivotal role in what to select for use; summer sees more porcelain used than stoneware as it imparts a feeling of coolness to the touch and is generally lighter in the hand. In the cold months more stoneware is used, such as Bizen or Shigaraki, the latter especially in autumn as the rusty clay body tones mimic the seasonal color. The most famous of all Japanese pottery for meals is Karatsu ware, used in any season.

Perhaps the most distinctive use is in a kaiseki meal, the multi-course repast that originated in Kyoto with imperial court cuisine. The kaiseki meal which precedes a way-of-tea gathering has been hugely influential in the way food is not only prepared but how it's served, even down to the lowly chopstick rest. A chopstick rest! Endless designs can be seen from dragons, flowers and fish to Hello Kitty.

Some Japanese pottery styles change over time with use, usually glazed wares such as Shino ware or Hagi. Named after a port down in Yamaguchi prefecture, Hagi ware was started by captured Korean potters in what has been termed the pottery wars of the late 16th century. Hagi wares are said to go through seven changes of color over time. In our kitchen we use a Hagi teapot that when brand new was uniformly buff-toned; now it has stains and spotty areas that make it difficult to believe it's the same pot bought just a few years ago. Hagi potters say you must raise your Hagi pottery just as you raise a child.

Pottery is such an important aspect of Japanese culture that in the 1950s the government enacted laws for the protection of cultural properties, and potters who contributed greatly to their respective styles were designated Living National Treasures. Bizen, located in Okayama prefecture, has five potters honored. The current Living National Treasure is Jun Isezaki.

> "How food is arranged in its serving dishes is particularly important. In essence it is the same as arranging flowers or painting a picture: one uses food to create an artistic design, combining colors and shapes like an artist."
>
> Japanese chef/artist Kitaōji Rosanjin (1883-1959)

Visiting regional pottery towns in Japan is always a delight, from the remote countryside of Oita prefecture in Kyushu known for its folky style Onta pottery to the semi-industrial town of Shigaraki, not far from Kyoto, the capital for 1,200 years. The pottery used in Kyoto is very different from the styles mentioned before, which are rural and influenced by the needs of an agricultural area. Kyoto pottery is heavily influenced by Chinese and Korean pottery of long ago and one can find painted porcelain or celadon in shops lining the road to Kiyomizu Temple, for example. The most famous of all tea bowl styles that originated here is called raku, the family name of a line of potters now in their sixteenth generation. Usually the bowls for matcha powdered green tea are either black or red as the frothy emerald color of the tea contrasts so well. Kyoto is the cultural capital of Japan and all the ancient kilns are from Nagoya in central Japan and extend west.

A meal can be more than simply nourishment for the body; it can nourish our spirits, root us in beauty and conversations will revolve around utensils, as well as the meal itself. I recall a meal with a person so enraptured with a sake cup that he turned it slowly in his hands and lost all sense of where he was and who he was with.

ROSANJIN described ceramic tableware as "kimino for food" and he went on to say, "How food is arranged in its serving dishes is particularly important. In essence it is the same as arranging flowers or painting a picture: one uses food to create an artistic design, combining colors and shapes like an artist."

Japan's culinary soul, the izakaya stands as testament to a profound love for food, drink and camaraderie. What sets this unique institution apart from its global counterparts?

Izakaya Culture

BRUSH ASIDE the noren shop curtains and rattle open the sliding door. Fumes of skewers grilling over red-hot coals assail the senses, while a burst of laughter fills the room. In the dimly lit space, a gruffly affable chef points you to a stool at the wooden counter. Soon after, the glug-glug of sake overflows its glass into a cedar box. This isn't just any eatery—it's an izakaya, the homey heart of Japanese gastronomic culture.

Envision a British pub's cosiness, combine it with the energy of a Spanish pintxos spot, sprinkle in the rustic authenticity of an Italian osteria, and season it with a dash of Danish bodega vibes. While each of these gathering points is cherished in their respective societies, the izakaya boasts customs and traditions that root it uniquely in Japanese culture. Found in countless numbers across Kyoto, from hole-in-the-wall standing bars like Ikura Mokuzai to the upscale Onikai (specialising in Kyoto vegetables), the izakaya is the beating heart of Japan's love for food and community.

The term izakaya combines the words *i* (to stay) and *sakaya* (sake shop), evoking a place to linger and indulge. Originating in the Edo period of the Tokugawa shoguns, the izakaya's inception was tied to Japan's embrace of commerce and the arts during an era of relative peace and stability, as well as isolation from the West. These establishments also have deeper historical roots; records speak of sake-serving precursors even in the courtly Heian epoch beginning in the eighth century.

As you sip your overflowing sake, absorbing the sounds, aromas and flavors, you realise that the izakaya is more than just a place—it's an experience, a tradition and a testament to Japan's rich culinary tapestry.

In Edo Japan, sake vendors began to offer seating to patrons, encouraging them to sample their brews onsite. As time went on, these establishments began to serve small accompanying dishes, known as otsumami, eventually transforming the modest sake shops into the vectors of conviviality we know today. Today there's an even closer cousin of the Edo period ancestor of the izakaya. Known as kaku-uchi, these are liquor stores that invite guests to enjoy a few standing-only drinks and nibbles (sometimes on vintage wine barrels) before closing up for the night. It's an unforgettable neighbourhood experience.

In the izakaya, at the counter or at low tables on tatami mats, patrons might initiate their gastronomic journey with draft beer and salty edamame. Almost de rigueur for a quality place is the o-tsukuri, beautifully presented sashimi of the utterly freshest catch of the day. This is followed by an ever-evolving selection of morsels such as shishamo smelt fish, munched from head to tail (with belly bursting with eggs) or tiny and delicate yari-ika squid, slathered in yellow miso. And of course, the ever-popular kara-age Japanese fried chicken or kushi-yaki skewers. Unlike the personal servings in pintxos bars or osterias, izakayas champion the art of shared dining, fostering a spontaneous camaraderie.

And izakayas aren't just for the convivial night out. They're also places of solace or contemplation, where one can slip in quietly, find a corner and enjoy an evening of solitary indulgence. The staff respects your space, making it equally welcoming for groups, couples and individual patrons. One of this writer's fondest memories are of evenings spent in an izakaya, in wintertime where the silence of the residential neighbourhood contrasted with the boisterousness of the crowd, leafing through a novel while soaking up the scene. Now and then dribbling sake from a hot atsukan flask. Even more than Parisian café culture, the izakaya is the quintessential place to appreciate la comédie humaine.

For according to Kenji Hashimoto, a sociologist at Waseda University who has extensively researched the izakaya culture, the cultural significance of the izakaya is fundamental. He calls it no less than "the mirror of [Japanese] society". The scholar notes that to truly understand a Japanese town's essence, one must visit its izakayas. Here, one discovers not just the flavors of local cuisine but the heart and soul of the community. Tales reminiscent of the Netflix drama *Midnight Stories* might come to life from Japan's subtropical Okinawa to the frosty reaches of Hokkaido.

Amid freedom and variety, certain conventions endure. The ritual often begins with an otoshi (in the Kansai region of Kyoto called a tsukidashi). It's a modest dish that sets the tone for the evening, serving as both a welcoming gesture and a subtle table charge. Custom dictates that you pour drinks for your companions rather than for yourself, a ritual that fosters bonding. And why does sake often overflow into wooden boxes or masu? This tradition, known as mokkiri, represents a gesture of generosity from the host. The overflowing sake, spilling from the glass into the masu below, symbolises abundance and goodwill.

Ultimately, what truly sets the izakaya apart is its communal atmosphere. Izakaya dining is all about sharing. Dishes are placed in the centre, where everyone partakes, fostering conversations and deepening friendship. Here people socialize and even chat with strangers around a counter or on low tables on tatami mats. These elements contribute to a homey ambiance, urging patrons to revel in a moment that lasts deep into the night. It's not just about eating and drinking; it's about celebrating life's simple joys in a setting that's uniquely and unapologetically Japanese.

The izakaya is a haven, a space to shed the weight of formalities and immerse oneself in the pleasures of food, drink, and camaraderie. According to Yoshiharu Doi, one of Japan's most noted food critics, the izakaya also becomes a place for people to find "a release from Japanese pressures of family or company life". It's where office workers find respite from rigid routines and where students relish post-activity gatherings.

The izakaya becomes a place where Japanese culture and cuisine seamlessly blend. Here, one finds unique experiences such as robatayaki, fire-side cooking, where diners select their desired ingredients from a counter, watching them get transformed over an irori hearth filled with hot coals, an evocation of now almost-vanished village culture. Or oden, where diners select their bowl from an assortment of fish cakes and vegetables in a large pot, all simmering in a fragrant dashi.

Food is only half (or sometimes less-than-half) of the equation. An izakaya's drinks menu is just as formidable, normally with a vast array of local shochu and sake, and other intoxicating pleasures. Moreover, these establishments will take an infinite variety of forms, from down-home to the avant-garde. Many modern izakayas, for example, in stylishly austere settings, specialize in pairing French natural wines with Japanese experimental dishes, a growing trend. One of the most notable is the Sakai Shokai in Tokyo's Shibuya district.

In Kyoto's maze of streets and alleys, Japan's izakaya culture comes to vibrant life in a symbiosis of past and present in the city's shitamachi downtown areas, perhaps reflecting yearnings for a simpler time. For the inquisitive and discerning traveler, there's a great deal more to discover than the refinement of temples, Zen gardens and tea houses. Kyoto has a wealth of intimate neighbourhood culture that those who are patient enough, and savvy enough will be able discover on leisurely strolls—not by guidebook but by the flaneur's inspiration.

For those who do, the handwritten daily fare and hanging drink flyers will open a unique universe of authenticity and tradition. They may recall scenes from a film by Yasujiro Ozu (who frequently featured salarymen washing away their cares in an izakaya.) Whether in Tokyo or Kyoto, one can be assured that this cosy ambiance eschews the Western norm of rapid table turnovers, instead endorsing hours-long soirées of conversation and culinary discovery.

As you sip your overflowing sake, absorbing the sounds, aromas and flavors, you realise that the izakaya is more than just a place—it's an experience, a tradition and a testament to Japan's rich culinary tapestry. Unified by a common convivial culture, the izakaya takes form in infinite variations, a place to enjoy unique local specialities. In the heart of Kyoto, where sometimes forbidding history permeates every corner, the izakaya stands in comforting counterpart, welcoming all with open arms and a promise of a memorable night.

The izakaya is a place where stories unfold, friendships blossom, and the weight of the world momentarily fades. To step into one is to immerse oneself in a microcosm of Japanese society, a place where history, gastronomy, and human connection converge, and where the simplicity of shared meals becomes a profound celebration of culture and camaraderie.

WORDS   AVA MEES LIST, HEAD SOMMELIER

Sake for Beginners

HOW TO READ A SAKE LABEL

1. Brewery name
2. Address
3. Category
4. 'Japanese Sake'
5. Rice variety + percentage
6. Description
7. Method
8. Logo

Welcome to the world of sake. Head sommelier Mees List has done all the hard work to guide you through the daunting array of choices and jargon. Kanpai!

WHO IS Junmai? Why does everyone talk about polishing percentage? Is hot sake always bad? How long can I age sake? How do I drink sake with friends? I feel you, my friend. The world of nihonshu, as sake is called locally, can seem overwhelming, intimidating and exclusive, but it doesn't have to be. You don't need to study extensively and it is easy to find simple tutorials on the web that can give you a little grip on the subject. However, here a few things I have learned along the way that can give you a little extra confidence and help you explore some different sides to this fantastic drink.

Start at Junmai. In fact, don't drink anything but.

A Junmai sake, quite simply put, is a sake without added alcohol. Why you would make or drink sake any other way is a mystery to me. It may sound impressive to ask for a Junmai sake off the bat, and I have actually had some people frown in surprise at my request (huh, this gaijin knows sake words), but in reality, this is just where you should kick off.

Explore less polished sake

Before rice grains are steamed, their outside is polished. This is because it is harder for the koji spore to permeate brown rice to start the fermentation. For many, the polishing of the rice grain, a time- and thus money-consuming process, has become such an obsession that there exist bottles with a 0% polishing rate, which basically means you are drinking a really expensive (USD 14,000 in a New York sushi restaurant) bottle made of rice powder. Whatever you wish, of course! Remember to pick some clothes from the emperor's wardrobe while you are at it. Jokes aside, letting go of the idea that a daiginjo, the polishing rate of at least half the grain, is the ultimate premium style opens up a different world of flavors, steering away from the perfumed floral sake into new depths. In fact, the less you polish the rice, the more rich and umami and complex a sake can become, as many of the grain's oils are found on the outside.

Drink some Atsukan

If you grew up like me, where hot sake was the plonk that accompanied the chewy maki rolls you plucked off a conveyor belt in your student days, there is no way you could think of drinking any more heated rice wine ever again. But many great sakes should be drunk at least at room temperature and express themselves amazingly once heated. Atsukan, the colloquial term for hot sake, can be found in many a restaurant and is served in a wide brimmed cup to cool it slightly and let the aromas free.

Try a koshu

Yep, sorry, really busting out the sake terms here. Koshu is sake that has been aged at least three years at room temperature. Sometimes this is done by the brewery, but often this is also something that happens at a bar, where bottles sometimes stand on shelves for years on end, developing into a deep, savory, dark and umami drink that tastes completely different from anything you've ever had before, except some quality tamari. Koshu is aged in bottles, not in barrels (taruzake, or barrel aged sake, is a completely different thing, with a strong taste of cedarwood). Following the development of the ageing is something you can do at home, if you are the patient type who can keep a bottle for years on end. Aged sake is a great pair with glazed barbeque sauces, toasted seeds or any kind of mushroom dish.

WHAT IS ATSUKAN?

Atsukan refers to a way of drinking where you pour the Japanese sake into a ceramic container called tokkuri and heat the tokkuri from the outside. The action of heating sake is called "kan wo tsukeru" or "okan" in Japanese.

1. Miwa in his cellar at Kumezakura Shuzo
2. Red rice for Ine Mankai
3. Samples before opening
4. Demonstration of kimoto making at Terada Honke

Keep your eye on your friends' cups

A general lesson in Japanese drinking etiquette also applies to sharing sake. In essence, the rule is as follows: make sure your friends' glasses are filled, but do not pour yourself. They in turn will look out for you, and so this shared ritual will take you through the night. Be careful though. Upon returning to your home country, you may find yourself constantly disappointed when no one cares for your empty glass, while at the same time your company might think you are trying to get them wildly drunk. This is a hypothetical situation of course. I wouldn't know anything about it.

WORDS　AYANOMIMI　ILLUSTRATIONS　PAULA TROXLER

Dos and Don'ts

Trains might be crowded but they are very quiet, taxis have automatic doors and Japan is a tipping-free zone. Here's a short helpful guide to manners and customs.

Do not talk on the phone on public transport. Texting is allowed, but talking on the phone is considered invasive and inconsiderate. Be respectful and quiet on all public transport.

Do not fold your hands when greeting. In Japan people bow when greeting. Place your hands either at your side or in front of your body.

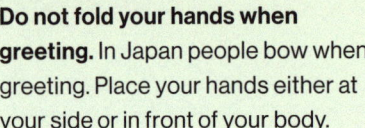

White rice is the chef's heart and soul. Let the chefs know in advance if you want a small portion of rice. In Japanese the word mottainai expresses the regret over waste, and leaving food is seen as bad-mannered.

Do not stick chopsticks in the rice. Lay them down or place them on the chopstick holder or pillow.

When eating sushi, do not dip the rice in soya. The rice will fall apart. Learn to enjoy the smell and taste of the rice itself.

Do not take food that smells on public transport. People are sensitive to smells, which also includes strong perfumes. Eating is only acceptable on long-distance shinkansen.

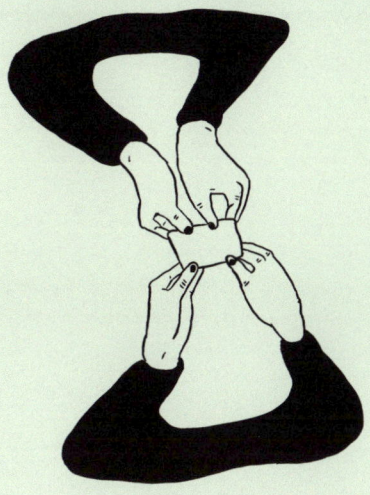

Give and receive with both hands. It is polite to use both hands when giving and receiving money, business cards, gifts and other things.

If gifts are offered, it is fine to accept them. And it is always acceptable to give a gift when visiting or meeting someone. The wrapping and ritual of presentation—with both hands—is important.

Do not close taxi doors. They open and close automatically.

Carry away your trash. There are very few public trash cans.

Lift bowls when eating. You should hold bowls of rice or soup in your hand when eating. Feel free to slurp your ramen loudly and with force.

Do not smoke while walking. Smoking in public is limited to designated areas.

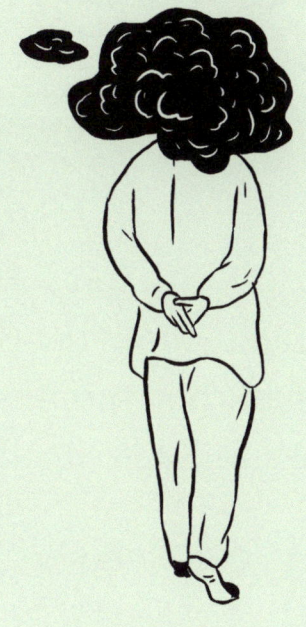

Do not walk barefooted. Always carry a pair of socks as you might be asked to take off your shoes at restaurants, shrines, historic buildings, traditional ryokan hotels and private homes.

Cover your shoulders. Formal wear includes clothing that covers shoulders and knees.

Make reservations for dining. It is advisable, and in some cases obligatory, to call ahead to book a table at a restaurant.

Do not feel you have to leave a tip. Tipping is not customary.

Don't hesitate to try the food in convenience stores such as Lawson, 7-Eleven or Family Mart. The onigiri are delicious.

Oshibori is for cleaning your hands. Not for wiping your face or to clean the table.

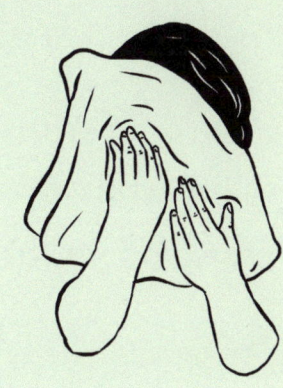

Do say "kanpai!" when you are drinking with someone.

Turn around after saying goodbye. It is polite to stay until the person who walks away turns a corner.

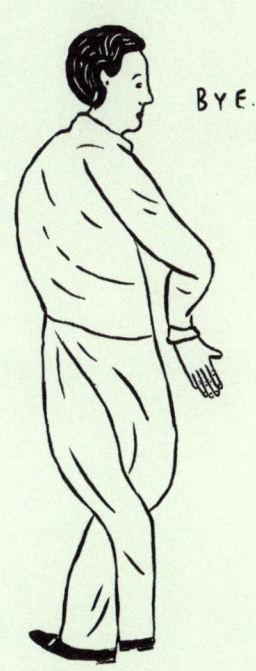

Hike Through History

Walk through crimson tori gates, climb the trail up the mountain and follow the steps of the marathon monks on a circuit that encompasses nature, culture and Kyoto itself.

Trees and nature are never far away in Kyoto and walking trails are easily accessible.

ONE OF THE MOST impressive hikers I've seen in Japan was a postman in Kyoto. It was during the pandemic, in September 2020. Japan had been shut down for nearly six months and we had no idea how long it would go on (another 24-plus months as it turned out). It was a surreal but wonderful time to be in the country. Covid numbers were low, the cities were mute. Kyoto was blissfully still, transformed into a little town of locals doing their local things, tending to their homes or businesses, buying and selling fruit and vegetables, cooking meals for regulars.

I walked Kyoto during this incredible hush and visited all the places I had ignored for a decade or more. I went to Kiyomizu-dera and Kinkaku-ji and Ginkaku-ji. To Mirei Shigemori's incredible moss garden at Tōfuku-ji. Places normally crushed by people, now empty. Eerily quiet. No selfie sticks, no TikTok-ing, no anything but the sounds of the temples themselves—monks chanting, sweeping, greeting each other, trees swaying, water falling.

Inspired, I walked further south down motionless lanes to Fushimi Inari Shrine, perhaps the most Instagrammed of all shrines. You know it immediately, that flowing rise of endless red torii gates. No place is more recognizable as a signal to say, publicly: I definitely went to Kyoto. But on this late morning in 2020 it was empty. So I started climbing, slowly up through them, up the considerable steps, up into the little warren of life that lives within the inner grounds. It was there I saw him, the postman. It had never even occurred to me that the shops above would receive mail, but of course they would. He carried his huge pack of letters, dressed in his uniform. September is still hot in most of Japan; I was soaked with sweat. He seemed somehow immune to the swelter. He smiled, greeted everyone by name, had little chats, handed over envelopes, bills, postcards, notes. It was a wonderful thing to witness. Though he wouldn't consider himself a hiker, he was. Each day he walked dozens of kilometers carrying his pack, saying hello, making sure the machinery of life continued.

FUSHIMI INARI, in its strange stillness, invited an exploration I had never done before. I started wandering the back of the small mountain on which it sits. I found a cluster of smaller shrines: Fushimi Inari Yotsu and Ganrikisha and Ichinomine at the top of Mt. Inari.

It was during this wander that I discovered the Kyoto

The mountains in which Kyoto is cradled are visible from most places in the city and along the 70-kilometre Kyoto Isshū trail, hikers can almost encircle the city and take in many of the temples along the route.

Isshū Trail, a 70-kilometer hodgepodge of routes circling most of the city. I had always admired the cradle within which Kyoto sat, the mountains visible in the near-distance from almost anywhere within the city. But I had never considered that a trail might connect them all, that you could circumambulate a large chunk of the city by foot, almost entirely in nature.

The south-eastern-most point of the Kyoto Isshū Trail actually finished at Fushimi-Inari, so I followed the trail north. It led through Sennyu-ji and back in the mountains up behind Kiyomizu-dera. It continued up, up, up into more mountains behind the Philospher's Path, up around the north edge of Ginkaku-ji, back into even deeper mountains on the north-eastern edge of the city, up to the famed Hiei Temple. The flora was lush, maples soon to turn, bamboo groves, evergreens. It was amazing to think about how close this all was to central Kyoto—only about 15 kilometers from Fushimi inari—but how far away it felt standing in the middle of Kawaramachi. This is one of many superpowers bestowed by a good walk; it gives context to relationships between seemingly disconnected locations. If subways and cars and buses chop up geography, walking stitches it all back together, provides a space for reflection and helps one understand why certain things were built in certain places.

MOUNT HIEI and its temple are home to the famous marathon monks who walk 40,000-plus kilometers over seven years as part of a religious practice to "clarify the mind and spirit." It takes 1,000 days. Only 46 monks have ever completed the challenge since 1885. When I first heard about this practice, I assumed it took place at some mountain in the hinterlands of Japan, somewhere tough to access, secluded, far away from the crowds and chaos of a city. But no, it was right here, right on the edge of Kyoto proper. Just a couple hours of strolling from the center of the city and you were with these great men. It was wild to imagine this extreme asceticism so close to Gion, to the bustle of gambling parlors and izakaya and college students wobbling arm-in-arm drunk along the Kamogawa.

I haven't participated in the 1,000-day challenge, but I have walked the 500-plus kilometers from Tokyo to Kyoto twice, taking about 30 days each time. The two old routes, the Nakasendō and Tōkaidō, intersect in Kusatsu, on the south-eastern edge of Lake Biwa, a few dozen kilometers outside of Kyoto. Both times, I've marveled at having completed the task, the surreal quality of having started at Nihonbashi in Tokyo and—by dint of simple step after simple step—traversing the whole distance between the two cities.

Walking from Kusatsu, you trace the southern edge of Lake Biwa and pass famed walker and Haiku poet Matsuo Bashō's grave in the district of Otsu. I always say hello before continuing up to the small mountain pass at Ōtani, past the old ichi-ri-zuka mile marker. These earthen mounds were built along all the old roads in the 1600s as a way to measure how far you'd gone in the day, each mound about four kilometers from the next. The standard was to walk about ten ri a day.

From there you walk through the nook of Yamashina Ward, a kind of valley village on the back side of Kiyomizu-dera. Now you're nearly back in Kyoto proper. I love the approach—it's quite ugly, like entering Kyoto via New Jersey. There's a realness to it that's delightful, especially knowing what lies beyond, the beauty and elegance of Kyoto itself.

The route takes you past the Miyako Hotel made famous by Truman Capote when he interviewed Marlon Brando

Just a couple hours of strolling from the center of the city and you were with these great marathon monks. It was wild to imagine this extreme asceticism so close to Gion, to the bustle of gambling parlors and izakaya.

Evergreens, maples, and bamboo surround hikers on the trails which are a walkable distance from the city.

there in 1957 for *The New Yorker*. Can you imagine, Kyoto in 1957? What a dream it must have been and not unlike, in many ways, the Kyoto of the pandemic years, quiet, almost forgotten. There in the Miyako, Brando sat in his Japanese-style suite, Capote watching him inhale steak and apple pie, a portentous gorging that would lead to the significantly larger Brando of later years. Eventually, leaving the interview in the middle of the night, Capote walks the streets of Kyoto: "But at two in the morning… the cabarets are shuttered; only cats remained to keep me company, and drunks and red-light ladies, the inevitable old beggar-bundles in doorways, and, briefly, a ragged street musician who followed me playing on a flute a medieval music. I had trudged far more than a mile when, at last, one of a hundred alleys led to familiar ground—the main-street district of department stores and cinemas."

I LIKE TO IMAGINE walking in Capote's steps when making this inglorious entrance into Kyoto. Down you walk, down towards Sanjyō Ōhashi, the bridge marking the end of the old roads, the counterpoint to Nihonbashi in Tokyo. But I don't stop at the edge of the bridge, I walk to the middle, to a historical mark that can be easy to miss: in one of the bridge's old iron ornamental caps, there is a gash. A gash from June 5, 1864, when a battle raged between Tokugawa Shogunate supporters and anti-imperialist Emperor supporters. Someone, during the melee, swung his sword and missed and hit that cap, marking it. It's a nice gash. And a simple reminder of how layered these streets are, how complex even the most seemingly simple of hikes around Kyoto can be. A postman delivers mail up the tiny mountains of Fushimi inari, weaving like a footballer between tourists on these post-pandemic "normal" days. A hiking route takes you quickly to the marathon monks of Mt. Hiei. And, if you're paying attention, the old historical roads into the city take you past an odd bit of Hollywood history, before dropping you off at a bridge where men once fought with swords over the future of the country.

The charming border of the Tatsumi Shrine on Shirakawa Minami-Dori

PHOTO: BEN RICHARDS

FOOD　　DRINK　　STAY　　ART　　DESIGN　　MARKETS　　FAMILY　　TEMPLES　　TRAVEL

KYOTO GUIDE

Welcome to our guide to Kyoto. The following is a selection of places the noma team loved while living in Kyoto during the winter and spring of 2023.

FOR THOSE of you who've not been to Japan before, you should know that restaurants are categorized very differently to the west where you might classify places into cheap, mid-range, or expensive. Here, restaurants are identified according to their specialties. One thing that is 100 percent certain: you need to plan your trip well. If you have restaurants that you really want to eat at when visiting, book well in advance. Thorough planning and research are crucial. While a simple Google search to identify a specific shop may fall short due to Japanese-only names or a lack of an online footprint, don't be disheartened. Some iconic restaurants may be challenging to access, but persistence can pay off. Yet, if you find yourself on a serene Kyoto alley, lured by the warm glow of an unmarked entrance, heed that call, trust your intuition, and step inside. You'll be glad you did.

In this guide you'll find some of our favorites from a variety of categories, from restaurants to wine bars, galleries to flea markets, and more. We truly hope that you will fall in love with Kyoto as much as we did.

FOOD

As the epicenter of Kaiseki cuisine, the former imperial capital has fed everyone from emperors to samurai, from the greatest artists to the finest artisans, and all others in between.

WITH PEERLESS ingredients and meticulous attention to detail you can eat like royalty in the tiniest hole-in-the-wall that has been tended by the same family for generations. Kyoto has not only some of the best Japanese restaurants in the country (although the meaning of what a Japanese restaurant encompasses a huge range), it has also welcomed dining traditions from around the world and culinarily speaking, is multilingual. The following list will offer some of our favorites, but we would need a novel to write about every single wonderful establishment in the city. As with travel anywhere, trust your gut, and be adventurous.

RAMEN

Hot broth typically with wheat noodles. The styles of broth vary as do the toppings.

SUGARI

Fun, delicious, casual, hole-in-the-wall ramen joint that welcomes everyone, but you might have to wait in line. Known for tsukemen dipping noodles or a rich pork-based, spiced ramen. Add on the charred beef intestine, it's delicious. There are four locations in Kyoto.

HONKE DAIICHI-ASAHI

Super delicious, fatty pork broth ramen, but expect a very long line. This place is popular.

VEGAN RAMEN UZU

Vegan ramen in a rather experiential setting. Reservations are needed.

RAMEN OYAJI

This very local spot opened in the late 70s. The family recipe is secret and well-protected. Order the Chashu-men.

RAMEN DAIKI

Old-school, well-respected ramen shop.

RAMEN TOUHICHI

This great ramen spot has a Michelin Guide Bib Gourmand rating. Known for the chicken shoyu ramen.

1

RAMEN NISHIKI

Small shop in Gion with sea bream-based broth.

RAMEN MUGYU VOL. 2 KARASUMA TAKOYAKUSHI

Down an alleyway, this ramen shop is known for its shio ramen and torisoba. A hidden gem.

3

5

2

4

6

1-4. Sugari
5. Ramen Mugyu
6. Ramen Touhichi

SOBA

Buckwheat noodles—the original Japanese noodle. Typically served cold with a cold broth for dipping, but also can be served hot in broth.

TEUCHISOBA KANEI

Lunch-only soba shop a little outside the center of Kyoto, which has a Michelin Guide Bib Gourmand rating.

MASUTOMI

Right next door to Sanmikouan, but a bit more famous. It serves both hot and cold soba.

SANMIKOUAN

Soba shop right by one of the tiny rivers in Gion. Known for its sudachi soba.

JUUGO

Arguably one of the best soba shops in the city. This soba master grows his own buckwheat and makes soba to order. Reservations are a must. Near the Philosophers Path.

SOBATSURU

Run by three jolly siblings, this place has excellent soba but don't overlook all the other great small dishes on the menu. They excel in warm sake to heat you up when it's cold outside—and if that is not enough, ask for some sobayu (the cooking liquid) to warm your hands.

SUBA SOBA

Suba Soba only serves hot soba in a no-fuss setting between the Kamo and the Takase River.

OBANZAI

Obanzai is a style of Japanese cuisine with its roots firmly in Kyoto. To be considered obanzai, at least half of the ingredients on a menu must be from or processed in Kyoto prefecture. It's a style of seasonal home cooking that strives to reduce waste and is often vegetable-focused, but sometimes includes protein.

OKAZUYA ISHIKAWA

Tranquil and traditional, this is a fantastic spot for obanzai in Shimogyo Ward.

ORYORI MENAMI

An 80-year-old restaurant focusing on home-style cooking, with a Michelin Guide Bib Gourmand rating. The people are warm and always smiling.

1. Sanmikouan
2-3. Juugo
4-5. Suba Soba

KYOTO GUIDE

164

PHOTO: CORY SMITH, KEISUI SUZUKI

IZAKAYA / SHOKUDO

Izakayas are an informal type of Japanese bar often serving a variety of food with a variety of drinks. Shokudos typically have a stronger focus on the food, but still offer variety.

ISO STAND

A cozy, two-floor izakaya right next to natural wine bar Deux Cochons. Great space, tasty food, delicious sake and natural wine. Get the clay pot rice and karaage. Call ahead for a booking.

SHOKUDO MIYAZAKI

A disciple of Shokudou Ogawa. Delicious and still possible to get a booking.

NIJO ARITSUNE

A slightly more refined izakaya, not an everyday type of place. The food is delicious and the atmosphere is interactive and lively.

SAMBONGI SHOTEN

Cozy izakaya with natural wines and a Michelin Guide Bib Gourmand rating. Fun spot.

BINGO

Very casual, small, with a lively environment. Enjoy the fun vibes and good times.

TO.

Tiny neighborhood spot, with an amazing mix of Italian and Japanese flavors. Great people working here. The wings are insane as is the risotto carbonara.

GION ROHAN

A famous and popular izakaya amongst tourists. A la carte menu with very good, very consistent food.

SHOKUDOU OGAWA

Counter-only casual restaurant that serves very high-quality food. Very difficult to book.

SAKABA IKURA MOKUZAI

Super casual stand-up izakaya with incredibly delicious food.

TSUNEYA DENSUKE

Another more refined izakaya, with a Michelin Guide Bib Gourmand rating. Family-run operation with a large menu, but full of deliciousness. Reservations are essential and well worth it.

BERANGKAT

Super cool little eatery with a Michelin Guide Bib Gourmand rating that serves Japanese ingredients but with a little more spice than you'd expect.

1-2 Shokudo Miyazaki
3.   Nijo Aritsune
4.   Bingo
5.   Sakaba Ikura Mokuzai

TONKATSU

Breaded and fried pork cutlet often utilizing the fillet or loin.

KARASEMITEI

Neighborhood spot just north of Nijō Castle. Warm and inviting.

KATSUKURA TONKATSU SANJO MAIN STORE

Great little shop in the Sanjo Meiten-gai Shopping Arcade. You make your own dipping sauce in a small mortar and pestle at the table. Very tasty.

GYUKATSU KYOTO KATSUGYU – KAWARAMACHI

Kyoto-style beef tonkatsu. Get here early; there is always a line.

TONKATSU ICHIBAN

South of the center, but one of the best tonkatsu in the city, and has a Michelin Guide Bib Gourmand rating. Well worth a visit.

GYOZA

Dumplings. Typically made with pork and garlic but varieties with chicken or vegetables can be found. Always a good choice with a frosty beer.

GYOZA CHAOCHAO

This is part of a chain, but the gyoza are quick, cheap, and tasty.

HAAAN!!

More of an izakaya with a strong focus on dumplings. Open late with plenty of cold beer.

EBISUGAWA GYOZA NAKAJIMA

Dumplings in a classic setting with punk rock on the speakers.

TAMAGOYAKI SANDO

Egg sandwich, essentially an omelet in between white bread.

MOMOHARU

Tiny cafe serving Tamagoyaki Sano (aka Japanese omelet sandos). The French toast is incredible too. Right next door to a hamburger shop.

YAKITORI

Grilled chicken skewers. All cuts of the chicken are used in yakitori and it's not uncommon for yakitori restaurants to serve some dishes with chicken cooked rare. Grilled vegetables are also a must with a Yakitori meal.

YANAGI KOJI TAKA

Tiny, but fun and lively yakitori spot with an incredible environment.

MIHANA

Such a warm and inviting yakitori spot. Great natural wine selection and Mika is such a wonderful host. Reservations are a must.

CHABUYA

Lively yakitori in a wonderful setting. It fills up quickly, so go early or make reservations.

HITOMI

Cozy yakitori spot with a Michelin Guide Bib Gourmand rating, just over the Kamo River. A favorite for many of the noma staff.

YAKITORI NISHINO

South of the center, but one of the best tonkatsu in the city, and has a Michelin Guide Bib Gourmand rating. Well worth a visit.

YAKITORI KAMINARI

Many businesses in Kyoto are small, but this one is particularly tiny. One man with tons of personality runs the show. You will smell deliciously of smoke after a meal here.

1. Tonkatsu Ichiban
2-3. Ebisugawa Gyoza Nakajima
4. Momoharu
5. Chabuya
6. Yakitori Kaminari

KAISEKI

Traditional Japanese fine-dining, tasting-menu format. The city is full of many different types of kaiseki restaurants from very traditional to slightly more modernized. Here we include a longer list because some of them might be more difficult to get into. If you can find your way into one of the traditional kaiseki houses for a lunch or dinner, it is well worth it.

ISSHISOUDEN NAKAMURA

Founded 180 years ago, the legendary three-Michelin star chef, Motokazu Nakamura is the sixth-generation owner-chef.

MIYAMASO

A bit out of the city, but a truly nature-driven experience, with two Michelin stars.

HYOTEI

In a 450-year-old building and run by the same family for 15 generations, this three-Michelin-starred kaiseki restaurant is about as traditional as you can get.

TOMINOKOJI YAMAGISHI

Chef Takahiro Yamagishi is a master of kaiseki and one of the best in Japan.

KYOTO KITCHO ARASHIYAMA

Third-generation owner Tokuoka Kunio is a legendary chef who has influenced many Europeans.

KIKUNOI HONTEN

Old school, ultra-traditional Japanese. There are a few kaiseki restaurants in Kyoto that are impossible to get into, and others that are barely possible to get into, but this is the best. It's like visiting Paul Bocuse in Japan. Kukunoi has 3-Michelin stars and chef Murata-san is literally The Don in Japan. Very traditional setting, but an incredible experience.

SOUJIKI NAKAHIGASHI

In a legendary spot next to the start of the Philosopher's Path, chef Nakahigashi comes from a long line of chefs (his brother runs Miyamaso), and Nakahigashi san is driven by foraging. Every day he picks food from the land and serves it to guests in a deep and meaningful way. Reservations are a must.

YUKIFURAN SATO

It's hard to put this restaurant in a category because it's not a traditional or formal kaiseki set-up. It is a tasting-menu format: chef Koichi Sato decides what to cook, you sit at the counter. Very hard to book, not listed in many guides, extremely good.

JIKI MIYAZAWA

Fantastic kaiseki meal by chef Takatomo Izumi, who also knows a thing or two (or three) about natural wines and sakes. One Michelin star.

KINOBU

Traditional one-Michelin star kaiseki under owner chef Takuji Takahashi.

OGATA

Possibly the hardest kaiseki reservation in Kyoto. With two Michelin stars it is considered one of the best in Asia right now.

1-2. Kikunoi Honten
3-4. Soujiki Nakahigashi
5. Ogata

FRENCH

LE BOUCHON

Another French bistro with delicious, classic French fare.

DEUX COCHONS

French, natural wine bar with smaller bites.

LE 14E

Outstanding, extremely tiny French bistro with a Michelin Guide Bib Gourmand rating. Go here if you are craving a good steak. Excellent wine selection as well. Reservations are essential.

CONTEMPORARY JAPANESE

MONK

A fantastic experience. It sits right on the Philosopher's Path. A pizza oven, farm fresh ingredients, and a ton of heart and soul. This tiny place is hard to get into, but worth the effort—you'll need some luck though.

TEMPURA MATSU

Despite the name, this is not a tempura restaurant. It's a very Japanese, informal setting, but with high-quality cooking by a young chef who took over from his late father a few years ago. Absolutely delicious.

LURRA°

A small, fantastic Michelin-starred counter restaurant helmed by former noma intern Jacob Kear that focuses on live-fire cooking. Don't miss the Sunday brunch when it happens! The omelet is outrageously good.

1. Le 14e
2-5. Monk
6-7. Tempura Matsu

PHOTO: YUKA YANAZUNE

KYOTO GUIDE

168

SUSHI

The combination of perfectly cooked rice and pristine seafood. Kyoto is not known for sushi, but here are a few places to experience something special.

SUSHI SAEKI

A warm and inviting sushi counter with an incredibly talented and young team. Reservations are essential.

AZUMA SUSHI

Sushi counter near Toyokuni-jinja Shrine. Japanese speaking is useful here, but they do have set menus to make it easier.

SUSHI SUZUKA

Husband and wife team, seven-seat counter, incredibly kind people despite a lack of English. The entrance is a polished and brushed copper door, so look for this.

SUSHI SAKAI

Hidden behind Nishiki Market, his tiny five-seater sushi counter owned by a couple feels like an Alice in Wonderland experience. There are no business signs, not even a very noticeable door, but inside is the warmth and wisdom you feel when stepping into your grandparent's home.

1-5. Sushi Saeki
6. Azuma Sushi
7-8. Sushi Sakai

ITALIAN

PIZZERIA DA CIRO

Another great woodfire pizza option, this one with a Michelin Guide Bib Gourmand rating.

OSTERIA IL CANTO DEL MAGGI

Del Maggio is a tiny hole-in-the-wall Italian place. The chef does everything himself—he spent a few years living and working in Tuscany and fell in love with the region. The cuisine is truly Tuscan and the restaurant has only 16 seats, so reservations are essential.

SALSICCIA! DELI

A little homemade sausage shop where you can eat a hearty meal on weekends with great wine. Everything in this place is repaired once, twice, thrice as Salsiccia does everything himself. His Instagram is worth following for the sausage illustrations alone.

PIZZERIA NAPOLETANA DA YUKI

Popular pizza place for very good reason—they have a Michelin Bib Gourmand. Stone-oven pizza made with love and attention. Ask for the wine list; this collage is a real labor of love with handwritten notes and photo cutouts.

CENCI

Tasting menu in a beautiful cavernous space unlike any other in Kyoto, that blends Italian and Japanese cuisine—what's not to love? There is a great tea pairing for those interested, and otherwise a very good wine list. Also has a Michelin Guide Bib Gourmand rating.

1

2

INDIAN

TADKA2

An incredible Indian restaurant in Nakagyo ward. Such an unexpected but delicious place.

3

4

CHINESE / TAIWANESE

TAIHO

Sichuan Chinese spot with spicy cuisine and vats of their own miso aging in the back. Casual with an iconic natural wines list. This legendary spot in Kyoto has a Michelin Guide Bib Gourmand rating.

CANTONESE RESTAURANT HOSEN

Very popular Cantonese spot with a line out the door all the time. Plan ahead.

551 HORAI

Insanely delicious steamed buns, but always a line.

XUEMEIHUA SAIKONTAN

Xiao Long Bao, black wood ears, hot pot, almond pudding are not to be missed here.

DIN TAI FUNG

The legendary Taiwanese dumpling spot is in the Takashimaya store on the third floor behind ladies' garments. Known for their a la minute soup dumplings. We know it's a chain, but they never disappoint.

1. Pizzeria da Ciro
2. Pizzeria Napoletana Da Yuki
3. Cenci
4. Tadka 2

SWEETS

GION MANJU

Tiny mochi shop that always has a queue. Everything is handmade and they only produce a limited number each day. Right next door to Masutomi soba.

KASHIYANONA WAGASHI

Confectionary shop in Shimogyo Ward specializing in mochi.

DEMACHI FUTABA

Exquisitely textured mochi with red beans. A local favorite northeast of the Kyoto Imperial Palace.

KAMEYA KIYONAGA

A confectionary shop in the same family for 17 generations, in Gion near the Yasaka Shrine, known for wagashi mochi.

ICHIMONJIYA WASUKE

Bask in history. This is a 25th-generation confectionary shop just north of Daitoku-ji Temple. Enjoy tea and aburi-mochi as it was had more than 1,000 years ago.

KAZARIYA

Across the street from Ichimonjiya Wasuke and comparatively younger—it was founded in 1637—Kazariya also specializes in aburi-mochi, which is mochi on a stick that has been grilled and dipped in a sweet white miso sauce. The lines are always long at both shops.

BAKERIES & CAKES

HITSUJI DOUGHNUTS

Very popular spot for doughnuts.

MAISON DE FROUGE

A small patisserie in the Nakagyo Ward which focuses on strawberry-based desserts. They have a small strawberry farm in Fukuoka, which supplies their strawberry needs.

KURS

Small bakery run by a couple who made bread for events and flea markets. They always had an incredibly popular stand in the markets, so they decided to open a shop themselves.

OVGO BAKE

Vegan bakery with delicious cookies.

SLŌ KYOTO

Great sourdough but more importantly, great sandwiches.

DOUGH

Just south of the Imperial Palace park. Well-baked sourdough if you are missing your gluten fix.

MALEBRANCHE KYOTO

A confectionary shop with a few locations around the city and known for their fluffy cheesecake.

1

2

3

4

5

6

7

8

1-3. Kashiyanona Wagashi
4-6. Kurs
7-8. Ovgo Bake

DRINK

The beauty of Kyoto is that it is absolutely jam-packed with beautiful little one-person-show bars with five seats and overwhelming whisky selections.

IT SEEMS like behind every door there is a wondrous little watering hole where you could drink infinite highballs and become part of the furniture. Because there is! We highly recommend going down the rabbit hole that is the Kyoto bar scene on your own and make friends with whomever is seated next to you using hands and feet and cheers.

One tip: Many wine bars do not have a wine list, meaning you are at the mercy of the person behind the bar. Do not panic or beg for rare bottles but give yourself over to this system. Sure, you can give an indication of grape variety or color or if you feel like having something fizzy, but for the most part, go with the flow.

PHOTO: CORY SMITH

WINE

KUMANO WINEHOUSE

A dear friend described Takuma and Shuya of Kumano Winehouse as always "gracefully sinking" while the bar keeps filling with regulars, more often than not industry, dishes keep piling up but they remain ever calm, not willing to speed up unnecessarily but never standing still. Whatever you do, one thing is very important: you need to order the omelette.

DUPREE

Restaurant owned by the people of Ethelvine. Here you can actually find a physical wine list – but you are much better off consulting Yuka, the sommelier, as she has excellent taste.

KOMOREBINO NATURAL WINE BAR

Tiny spot with an incredibly kind owner. Plenty of wine variety here.

CHICHI KYOTO

An ice cream shop, gallery, and wine bar all in one. An unlikely combination, but it works so, so well.

CHROME

Wine bar and restaurant between Nijo Castle and the Imperial Palace.

ESTRE

Charming wine bar with plenty of food to go with, but they really focus on the wine.

TAGIRI

Tiny tiny Gion karaoke bar serving Italian natural wines. Our staff may or may not have ended late here on occasion.

ETHELVINE

Natural wine shop for bottle takeaway.

1. Dupree
2. Chrome
3. Tagiri
4. Kumano Winehouse
5. Ethelvine

SAKE

SAKE BAR YORAMU

A wonderful sake bar in a quiet neighborhood. The owner is an expat from Israel and has been living in Japan for more than 30 years. Amazing character and knowledge of sake. There are only about eight seats here. No reservations.

ETHELVINE

Besides a great natural wine shop, Ethelvine sells Kumezakura and Nichi Nichi as well as Terada Honke.

UEDA LIQUOR STORE

Find the excellent aged sake of Kinoshita at Ueda Liquor Store. Their 2017 Stork Label was heated and poured on our pairing for a while. The shop is pretty far from the city center, but on your way back into town you can eat the entire menu and drink hot sake at the number one spot Sobatsuru. You won't regret either of these undertakings.

JAM + SAKE BAR

A favorite among noma staff after the Tokyo popup. Wonderful people run this place with delicious sake.

UKAI SHOTEN

The best place to find sake in Kyoto is Ukai Shoten. It is kind of out of the way, Michiko-san does not speak English and the shop may be closed when she is picking up the kids from school, but do not be deterred, the selection is fantastic. Don't skip the second room where you can find the aged sake, and make sure to open the fridge and get some of the unpasteurized bottles. Once there I found a cloudy sake made by Moriki Shuzo that was so explosive it was bottled in a plastic soda bottle and it took about fifteen minutes to open without detonating. It was probably the best doburoku I ever had. Ukai Shoten is also the purveyor of Mukai Shuzo, maker of the infamous Ine Mankai red rice sake.

BEER

DIG THE LINE BOTTLE & BAR

Craft beers, both Japanese and foreign. Eight taps as well as cans and bottles from around the world.

CRAFTMAN

A sneaky cool craft beer spot with 40 taps of mainly Japanese beer. Stand at the front bar or stay for small plates and beer. A gem of a spot.

BEER PUB TAKUMIYA

The liveliest of beer spots. A lot of fun and a party every night. Great for small bites. Sit at the bar.

HACHI RECORD SHOP AND BAR

The opposite of Takumiya. Very mellow, very small. Usually playing obscure Japanese jazz. Record shop on the second floor. Absolutely worth the visit.

KYOTO BREWING CO.

Kyoto Brewing Co. can be found all over town, but beer always seem to taste better from the source.

1. Jam + Sake Bar
2. Sake Bar Yoramu
3. Ukai Shoten
4. Beer Pub Takumiya
5. Hachi Record Shop and Bar
6. Kyoto Brewing Co.

COCKTAILS

CHEZ QUASIMODO

After a career running a small neighborhood vegetable shop in the Nakagyo Ward, the owner of the space decided to skip retirement, convert the shop into a bar, and teach himself how to bartend. Stepping into this bar is completely transportive to a bygone era. The record player is always spinning with jazz playing through a vintage McIntosh receiver and crisp Tannoy speakers. Get a martini, sit back, and enjoy.

BAR K-YA

Intimate and dimly lit bar with great atmosphere in a traditional house. Cocktails featuring freshly squeezed fruit juices and a huge selection of single-malt whiskies.

L'ESCAMOTEUR

A bit of a younger place, but all the seriousness of professionals. High-quality cocktails in a lively environment.

CAFÉ/BAR OIL

Top floor of an apartment building complete with a terrace full of seats, a vintage Wurlitzer, Fender Rhodes, upright Steinway and a beautiful Telecaster. It's one big bar with some smaller tables and the owner is no-nonsense. Classic cocktails only. The environment is fantastic and the record player is always spinning.

GEAR

Owner wears a leather cowboy hat and takes no bullshit—but he does make a killer highball and John Lee Hooker is playing on the record player, so all is well.

KAZUBAR

A true hidden gem. Walk down a small side street off Kawaramachi-dori, and then down an even smaller alleyway. The bar is a few floors above Elephant Factory Coffee and is entirely lit by candlelight. Great music, good drinks and a truly unique vibe.

BAR LE COQ

Very cool and calm cocktail bar in a quiet neighborhood. Miles Davis on the record player and a wide variety of Japanese whiskies.

MITCH MITCHELL

A second floor bar named after Jimi Hendrix' drummer, great place for highballs and blues records, right by the main shopping center.

1. Chez Quasimodo
2. Bar Le Coq
3. Kazubar
4. Bar Le Coq
5. Gear

COFFEE

STYLE COFFEE

The owner Kurosu-san has spent his career thus far learning about coffee from a multitude of perspectives. His exploration took him to Melbourne, where he worked in the vibrant coffee scene, before spending some years under Masahiro's tutelage at Weekenders. He is an active member of the coffee community in Kyoto, and his micro-roastery is beloved among all.

WEEKENDERS COFFEE TOMINOKOJI

The great Weekenders. Tiny coffee shop in the back of a parking lot. A tiny oasis.

WEEKENDERS COFFEE ROASTERY

The roastery for Weekenders. A beautiful spot only open on Saturday and Sunday.

CLAMP COFFEE SARASA

A little cozy café where you can also get some breakfast-like lunch. Next to it is a little antique store and a flower shop.

KURASU

Visit them at their Kyoto Stand shop, close to the train station, or their Ebisugawa location, which is more focused on home brewing and coffee equipment. In this little space, designed to look like a domestic kitchen, they serve coffee made on the home brewing equipment that they sell in-store.

1-2. Weekenders Coffee
3. Kursau
4-6. Tarel

TAREL

Wine bar by night, cafe by day. This little shop, set in a shipping container, is run by a lovely chap called Mossan, a true jack of all trades. Between serving wine and coffee (from Switch coffee roasters in Tokyo), he also bakes the bread they serve, right behind the very same tiny counter space.

ARCHI COFFEE AND WINE

A bit west from the center of Kyoto lies this sleepy shop complete with tatami mats and snacks.

COYOTE

Located close to Kyoto station, Coyote is a coffee roastery offering a limited food menu. Grab a quick bite before heading off on the Shinkansen or simply come to enjoy some genuinely tasty vegan fare.

TEA

TEAROOM TOKA / GALLERY NICHINICHI

Intimate, six-seat tearoom located in a century-old house in the heart of Kyoto that works with organic farmers from all over Japan. Tea is served in beautiful, hand-crafted ceramics which are also on display in the gallery upstairs. In the Hakudo tea tasting, you can compare different teas and try some accompanying Japanese sweets. The gallery is well worth visiting.

ZERO WASTE KYOTO

This zero-waste grocery store has a wonderful secret in its attic. In this tatami-floored space owner, Mutsumi, offers sauna treatments accompanied by herbal infusions. From time to time, visiting practitioners deliver treatments. Mutsumi holds a wealth of knowledge about her herbs and is usually very excited to share it.

FARMOON

An architectural gem hidden in a suburban neighbourhood of Kyoto, where you can sample teas from the Tsukigase estate, a 17th-generation natural tea farm based in Nara. At night this turns into a cozy restaurant with an incredible vibe.

IPPODO TEA

Ippodo has served high-quality Japanese tea for nearly three centuries. Knowledgeable staff will guide you through their selection, which includes matcha, sencha, gyokuro and bancha, all grown locally.

1-3. Tearoom Toka / Gallery Nichinichi
4-5. Ippodo Tea

PLACES TO STAY

Staying in a ryokan is the perfect introduction to Japanese hospitality and the subtle gestures that make guests feel at ease. The calm austerity of the tatami mats and shoji screens, the comfort of the futon and the enveloping quilts, and the discreet service are replicated in other ways in other forms of accommodation, but all will leave you feeling cared-for and appreciated. However, for those that seek the comfort of western abodes, Kyoto offers plenty of options.

KYOTO FOUR SISTERS RESIDENCE

More casual serviced apartments owned by a lovely couple.

TAWARAYA RYOKAN

A 300-year-old ryokan in the heart of Kyoto, known for their omotenashi.

R&RUN SERVICED APARTMENTS

Sleek and extremely comfortable serviced apartments hidden in the center of the city.

ACE HOTEL

Our home for the Kyoto popup and a wonderful place to stay.

HANARÉ MACHIYA GUEST HOUSES

Stay in ultra-traditional but beautifully renovated townhouses in the best parts of Kyoto.

1-2. Hanaré Machiya Guest Houses
3-4. Ace Hotel

PHOTO: YOSHIHIRO MAKINO

ADVERTORIAL – KYOTO CITY TOURISM ASSOCIATION

ENJOY KYOTO ALL YEAR ROUND

No matter when you visit Kyoto, you will find things to do and see including culture, art, nature.

Festivals and seasonal events are held daily throughout the city. Many of these unique celebrations date back hundreds, and even thousands, of years and offer fascinating insights into the history, culture and customs of the old imperial city.

PHOTO: BEN RICHARDS

FESTIVAL HIGHLIGHTS

AOI MATSURI
MAY 5
This elegant and ancient hollyhock festival dates from some 1,500 years ago. More than 500 people dressed as Heian aristocrats, parade from the Kyoto Imperial Palace, past the Shimogamo-iinja Shrine to the Kamigamo-jinja Shrine.

GION MATSURI
JULY 1-31
One of the three major festivals in Japan and a UNESCO Intangible Cultural Heritage. Rituals and events are held over the month, but the Yamahoko Float Processions are on July 17 and 24, when 34 gorgeously decorated floats, some enormously tall, are hauled through the city. Yoiyama Festival (July 16) is a preview of the float parade and offers glimpses into homes and shops.

GOZAN NO OKURIBI
AUGUST 16
"Flames of Prayer Floating" is a Buddhist event to send off the spirits of the ancestors. Enormous bonfires in the form of Japanese characters – Daimonji, Left Daimonji, Myoho, Funagata and Torii – are lit on the hillsides surrounding Kyoto.

JIDAI MATSURI
OCTOBER 22
This procession celebrating the founding of Kyoto, depicts the history of Japan with some 2,000 participants dressed in accurate costumes from every period. The parade stretches almost 2 kilometers as it marches from the Imperial Palace to the Heian Shrine.

KYOTO 2024 ATTRACTIONS

JANUARY
Hatsumode, first shrine visit of the New Year

FEBRUARY
Setsubun, Kyoto Marathon

MARCH
Hanami, cherry blossoms

APRIL
Miyako Odori, performed by geiko (geisha) and maiko

MAY
Fujimori Matsuri, Imamiya Matsuri, Saga Matsuri, Mifune Matsuri

JUNE
Kawayuka, riverside summer terrace

JULY
Morning time at temples and shrines are specially recommended

AUGUST
Kyo no Tanabata, Star Festival, held in July elsewhere, but in August in Kyoto

SEPTEMBER
KYOMAF, Kyoto International Manga Anime Fair

OCTOBER
Kurama no Hi Matsuri, same day as the Jidai Matsuri

NOVEMBER
Autumn foliage

DECEMBER
Jyoya no Kane and Omisoka, New Year's Eve

ART

Beyond its history and iconic temples, Kyoto is a dynamic metropolis brimming with art and design, and amid the bustling tourist attractions, it's easy to overlook the vibrant local art scene and its excellent museums. Art and design infuse every aspect of Kyoto but remember that this city operates on its own time, demanding patience and appreciation. To truly experience Kyoto's authenticity, immerse yourself in its rhythm, savor its artistry, spaces, and natural surroundings, and let the city surprise you. Kyoto is not a city where you come to demand an experience; it's a place where your genuine interest will open doors you could never imagine.

STARTING near Kyoto Station in the south, a visit to the **Kyoto National Museum** is highly recommended for those eager to grasp Japan's and Kyoto's ancient capital essence. Dating back to 1897, it is one of Japan's oldest museums and among the few designated top-level national museums in the country. The museum's exhibitions are housed in the Heisei Chishinkan, a modern building opened in 2014, designed by Taniguchi Yoshio, known for his work on New York's Museum of Modern Art.

From here, head to **POJ Studio (Pieces of Japan)**, a close neighbor of the museum. This gallery and store showcases the work of Japan's next-generation traditional artisans. The carefully curated space is replete with authentic and affordable items, every piece meticulously chosen for its aesthetic beauty and functional excellence, demonstrating the mastery passed down through generations. It's the perfect place to find a cherished keepsake from Japan. If time permits, indulge in a kintsugi workshop in-store, or for those who want to stay longer in Kyoto, POJ Studio offers a two-month intensive apprenticeship program consisting of 100 hours of kintsugi. You can also enjoy coffee in a bright and welcoming cafe around the corner from the studio.

Check out the schedule of exhibitions at the **Kyocera Museum**, established in 1933 and Japan's oldest public art museum, its classical facade set in the picturesque Higashi-yama landscape. Recently the Museum underwent revitalization by Japanese architects Aoki Jun and Nishizawa Tezzo, who preserved its classical elements while injecting fresh vitality into the Museum.

PHOTO: TRACI PAGE MORRIS

1. Kyocera Museum
2-4. POJ Studio
5. KYOTOGRAPHIE International Photography Festival

2

3

4

5

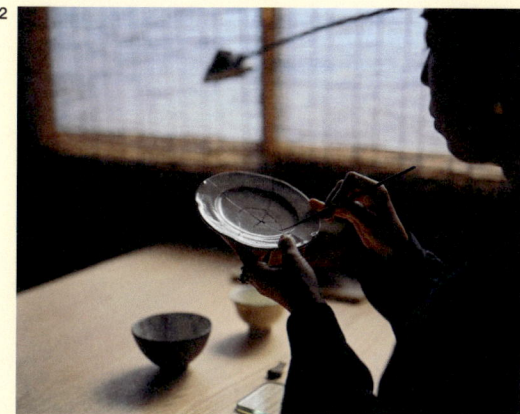

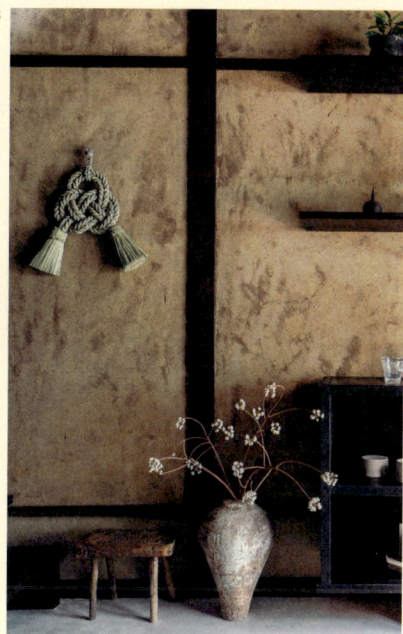

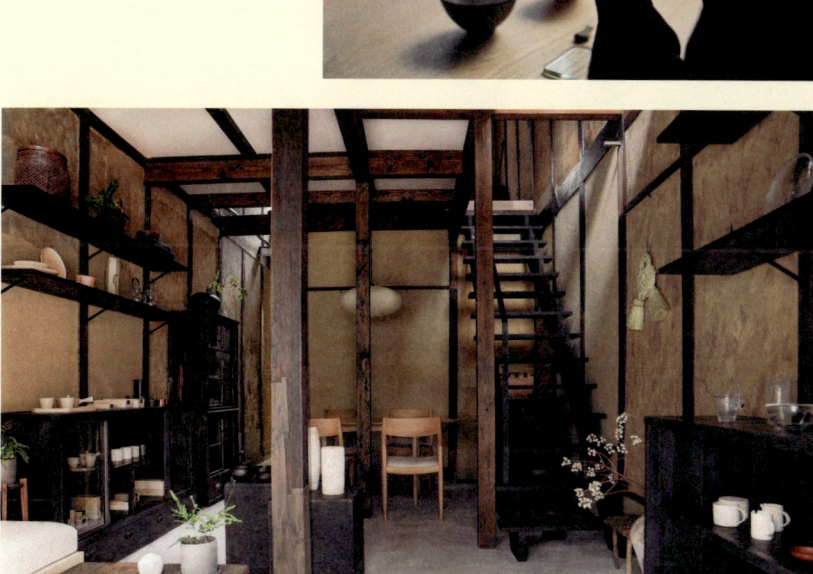

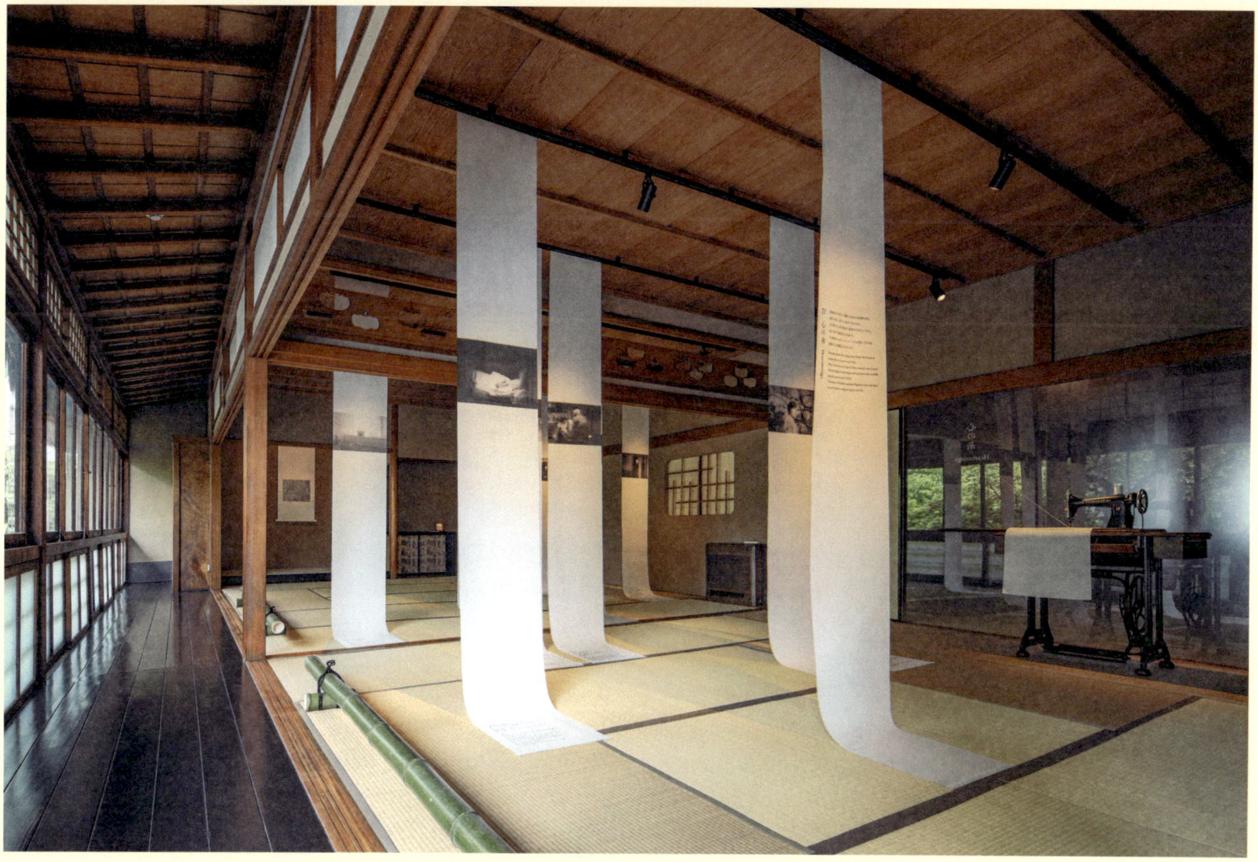

PHOTOS: MITSURU WAKABAYASHI. KAZUHIKO MATSUMURA, HACHIKU-AN, PHOTO BY GENRYOU GU, COURTESY OF KYOTOGRAPHIE

While heading north to explore Gion and Higashiyama, check out **Sokyo**, nestled within a cluster of antique stores and galleries. Sokyo specializes in ceramics and figurative sculptures, pushing the boundaries of traditional ceramics.

Cross the river and find **VOU**, an independent brand store and gallery. It's a treasure trove of one-of-a-kind items intertwined with contemporary culture. Finding the entrance may be tricky, but the unique discoveries make it worth the search.

Kyoto Art Centre, housed within a former Meiji-era elementary school hosts various activities, from exhibitions and concerts to traditional stage performances and dance events. Explore the building, part of which is designated as a tangible asset of Japan.

Heading northwest from Kyoto Art Center toward Nijo Castle, be sure to visit **Purple.** Created by Akaakasha and Seigensha, both specialists in art, design and photography publishing, it boasts an extensive collection of photography books and a gallery for exhibitions and events.

Heading north, discover **Delta** cafe and gallery, nestled in one of Kyoto's oldest shopping arcades. It provides a refreshing escape from the crowds of the central Nishiki market and offers a unique confluence of Kyoto's two rivers. Delta is the permanent space for the **KYOTOGRAPHIE International Photography Festival**, an annual spring event that curates photographic works spanning genres, styles, and themes, with site-specific-designed exhibitions in temples, culturally significant sites, and modern buildings.

In 2023, Kyotographie introduced a sister event, the **KYOTOPHONIE Borderless Music Festival** that offers concerts across the city, often featuring intimate shows performed exclusively for the festival. The roster includes an eclectic global mix of artists.

The last stop northwest is **Kanegae**, a beautiful gallery in a renovated traditional townhouse with an exceptional rotation of artists and an impressive collection, with works that range from antiques to contemporary art.

1. VOU
2. Kanegae
3. Sokyo
4. Purple
5. KYOTOGRAPHIE International Photography Festival
6. KYOTOPHONIE Borderless Music Festival

PHOTO: YURIKO TAKAGI, NIJO-JO CASTLE NINOMARU PALACE DAIDOKORO KITCHEN AND OKIYODOKORO KITCHEN PHOTO: KENRYOU GU, COURTESY OF KYOTOGRAPHIE. YUKA IWAHASHI, SALIF KEITA (TRIO), KOMYO-IN ZEN TEMPLE, COURTESY OF KYOTOPHONIE

TRADITIONAL PERFORMANCES

OCHAYA SHIGEMORI

An ochaya is literally a term for a tea house but is now known as a place to attend a traditional geisha or maiko performance. Ochaya Shigemori presents one of the most beautiful geisha performances in Kyoto.

MIBU KYŌGEN

A 700-year-old, traditional pantomime performance at Mibu-dera temple which is free to the public and performed in February, April, May, and October.

WORDS THOMAS LYKKE, CO-FOUNDER OEO STUDIO

DESIGN

Kyoto is a city that we at OEO Studio love to explore, the street kitchens and the contrast between old and new, which somehow works in its own mysterious way. Japanese aesthetics and architecture and the writings of authors such as Jun'ichirō Tanizaki are some of the many reasons we are drawn to Japan. Japanese woodwork is fascinating; with sashimono, you can construct anything from buildings to small objects using the same techniques by cutting and joining wood in simple or complex ways without the use of nails. Traditional Japanese houses with all their crafts and mastery are truly welcoming. Kyoto is an embracing city in every aspect and a place of great creative tradition.

PHOTO: KOTARO TANAKA

1.

2.

ASAHIYAKI SHOP & GALLERY

This tea pottery and gallery store located in Uji, is a 35-minute journey outside Kyoto in the oldest tea-producing region of Japan. For more than 400 years, Asahiyaki has specialised in ceramics and porcelain with exquisite coloured glazing. Easily reached by train or taxi.

Open 10:00–17:00
Closed Mondays

KAIKADO STORE & WORKSHOP

Kaikado dates back to 1875. The signature product is a tea caddy highly appreciated for its splendid style and functional, airtight design.

Open 9:00–18:00
Closed Sundays

HOSOO FLAGSHIP STORE AND GALLERY

Hosoo is a Kyoto-based textile company founded in 1688. Serving as its new headquarters, the building includes Hosoo's flagship store and a gallery with architectural emphasis on conveying the cultures of dyeing, weaving and kimono-making.

HAYAKAWA HAMONOTEN

A small and traditional shop with knives, kitchenware, and sharpening services.

ESSENCE GALLERY STORE IN KYOTO

A beautiful gallery with ceramics for daily life with a focus on tea rituals.

Open 11:00–18:00
Closed on Mondays

KAIKADO CAFE

The cafe is a 10-minute walk from the Kaikado Store and Workshop. OEO Studio worked with the Yagi family and a local architect to transform a 100-year-old city tram depot into an eclectic universe of coffee and tea.

Open: 10:00–18:30
Closed on Thursdays

ICHIZAWA SHINZABURO HANPU

Shinzaburo Ichizawa's family has been making durable canvas bags since 1905. Today, Ichizawa retails a colourful array of bags and heavy-duty aprons.

ARTS & SCIENCE

A multi-brand store with clothing, design objects and accessories.

RAINMAKER KYOTO

Founded in 2012 by designer Kohichi Watanabe, Rainmaker Kyoto elevates modern ready-to-wear to include the serene hallmarks of Japanese design.

HŌRIN-JI TEMPLE

Better known by the name of Daruma-dera, this temple showcases a collection of about 8,000 donated daruma dolls. Hōrin-ji also has a small Zen garden, offering a peaceful haven away from the bustle of the city.

1. Asahiyaki Shop & Gallery
2. Kaikado Store & Workshop
3. Hosoo Flagship Store and Gallery
4. Essence Gallery Store in Kyoto

WORDS — CHRISTINE RUDOLPH, NOMA RESIDENT STYLIST

FLEA MARKETS

One of the best ways to discover a new country is to visit its flea markets. While mingling with locals in a casual, friendly environment you learn about the culture and its history, get a sense of the fashion by looking at fabric and clothing, and understand the colors and materials that are used in everyday households.

1

PHOTO: TRACI PAGE MORRIS, CHRISTINE RUDOLPH

WE ARE DRAWN to local markets for many reasons but the most important are to see interesting things from another culture and help support local artisans.

Kyoto has flea markets scattered around the city with an amazing variety of items on offer, selling everything from fabric and clothing to rare collectibles, ceramics, artisanal crafts, secondhand furniture and often fresh food. And the locations are also amazing, many of them in the beautiful surroundings of famous temples and shrines.

These markets have been conducted for decades and a monthly excursion for many of the city locals is a long-standing tradition. Unlike Scandinavia, where markets are often held on weekends, in Kyoto they are held on a certain dates each month. Another difference is how the vendors showcase their items, always with style, order and practicality. This doesn't make the hunting less fun, on the contrary you can find inspiration just looking at the items displayed and how they are displayed. It's a stylist's dream!

Nothing beats an early morning at a flea market! Most markets open at sunrise, so the usual advice applies: go early to make sure you don't miss out and avoid the crowds.

Some vendors don't speak English but don't let that intimidate you. Japanese people are extremely helpful and fun, and we found a small notebook and a pen handy; the seller can write the offer and you can give thumbs up or write your offer back. Haggling is ok so long as is done with a smile and positive attitude. Prices are generally lower than at the average antique shops found in Kyoto, and often a lot lower.

TO-JI TEMPLE, KOBO ICHI MARKET

This flea market takes place on the grounds of UNESCO World Heritage-listed Koji Temple, an incredible backdrop for your shopping. The stalls are a mix of antiques, local handcraft, ceramic, artisan pieces, and food. Look out for bonsai trees and moss.

21st of each month
06:00-16:00
1,200-1,300 stalls

At the same venue but on a much smaller scale and not as well-known is the Garakuta-ichi market. Garakuta means rubbish or junk, and this market specializes in antiques. The stalls are in the west and south of the Toji temple.

First Sunday of every month
06:00-16:00
350 stalls

HEIAN ANTIQUE MARKET

Held in the Okazaki-koen Park in front of Heian Shrine, this is by far the hippest market, and the one that carries the most edited antiques. Here every booth is curated in that Japanese simple way: perhaps some small ceramic pieces on an old metal sheet as background; a booth made by hanging beautiful vintage indigo linens, floating in the wind as wall dividers. Young beautiful people in linen indigo wraps and long shirts are everywhere. This market definitely attracts people with style—excellent for people-watching.

10th of each month, but subject to change so check website.
09:00-16:00
250 stalls

The Heian Raku Ichi craft market is held in front of the Heian Shrine on the second Saturday of each month but is subject to change.

KITANO TEMNANGU SHRINE, TENJIN ICHI MARKET

Hundreds of vendors set up across the grounds and in the surrounding streets of this famous shrine to sell a wide variety of daily goods and antiques. The fair is held to commemorate the birth and death of the enshrined deity, Sugawara no Michizane. This market feels slightly more touristic than the Koji Temple one, but this still has amazing items on offer, especially in the smaller side streets, where it seems like people come from the outskirts of Kyoto with a load and are not professional dealers. There are real bargains to find here.

25th of each month
06:00-16:00
1,000 stalls

1. To-ji Temple, Kobo Ichi Market
2. Kitano, Tenmangu Shrine Street Market
3-4. Heian Antique Market

TRAVELING WITH FAMILY

Batting cages, anime, fluffy pancakes, amusement parks, stepping stones, karaoke and entertainment arcades. There's no shortage of things to do in Kyoto—and the kids will enjoy it too.

PHOTO: ICHI NAKAMURA

KYOTO is a fantastic place to visit as a family: people are friendly, it has a way of feeling calm even when it is busy, it is easy to get around and somehow it just seems like there is more time Kyoto than in many other places in the world. You can find everything in Kyoto. Walking around in the different areas of town you will see temples everywhere and every week there is a flea market at one of the temples in the center of town–see the directory for an online schedule.

Many of the bigger temples that you might have seen in movies or magazines are outside the city and extraordinarily beautiful. If you are jet lagged and up early, you can catch the train and be among the first people there by 7:00 before the swarms of people.

Amusement parks are also only a quick train ride away, while in the city there are arcades, batting cages, shopping, anime, nature, convenience stores, drug stores, coffee, and every type and style of restaurant you can imagine.

Our family was fortunate enough to spend five months in Kyoto. To have those great days as a family, we ensured that there was a balance between what the kids wanted to do and would enjoy, but also what the parents think is fun. In our family we have three daughters aged 9, 12 and 15 and I asked them each to plan the perfect family day that they would recommend to their best friends if they went to Kyoto.

DAY 1 – RO, 9

"I like that Kyoto is very safe, so I am allowed to do more things on my own there."

FLUFFY PANCAKES and tea for breakfast. Most kids love pancakes in any form, but there is something extra special about these huge pillowy, fluffy pancakes that brings the same joy as a birthday cake with candles. Most of the bigger hotels have fluffy pancakes on the breakfast menu and there are places all over town that serve them.

Taxi to a batting cage for a few hours. The Japanese love baseball and it is one of the biggest sports in the country. You see children and adults playing baseball when out walking and there are several batting cages about 20 minutes by car from the city center. Batting cages are not unique to Japan but it's a great experience for someone from Europe where baseball is not so big. Before you step into the cages, buy a card with as many rounds as you would like and simply swipe the card and go. Drinks, ice cream and small snacks are available.

It was so much fun that we didn't stop playing until we couldn't grip or swing the bat anymore.

After all the swinging, it's time for lunch. Head to the Kamo River that runs through Kyoto with beautiful walking paths, bicycle tracks and grass to sit on under trees. Stop at a convenience store, Family Mart or Lawson, and buy lots of onigiri, triangles of rice wrapped in nori seaweed with different flavors in the center. The packaging of this genius on-the-go lunch snack is as amazing as the onigiri itself. Follow the simple opening instructions to enjoy the soft moist delicious rice with a center of your choosing and crisp seaweed. The convenience stores have huge selections of cold drinks and nuts along with preserved and pickled treats. Crispy pickled plums are a favorite.

At the river make sure to choose a spot where there are stepping stones, some carved as turtles. The kids had a lot of fun running to the other side of the river and the water is no deeper than mid-shin.

After relaxing for a while at the river, walk to one of the many yakiniku restaurants where you grill meat yourself in the center of the table (there is also a large selection of vegetables). At some of the yakiniku restaurants you order from an iPad with a menu in English, which the kids thought that was great fun, but not as much as the fun of cooking their own food at the table and wanted to grill for everyone.

DAY 2 – GENTA, 12

"Everything is just better in Japan. Also I met my best friend in the whole world Nina at Kyoto International School and I miss her. We had so much fun in Kyoto."

IF THE WEATHER is good, take the Keihan line train to Hirakata-kōen station and walk five minutes to Hirakata Park, an amusement park established in 1910. It is surrounded by nature and the rides are lots of fun. If you go when it is warm, there is a cooling maze that is easily completed. A lot of people come to the park dressed in cosplay and even if your children are not into anime it is incredible to see. If anime is a thing in your family, it's likely you will see people dressed brilliantly as favorite characters and they are more than happy to take photos with you. Like all amusement parks there is an array of food and drinks, but to be honest, they are so much better in Japan.

After a good five hours or so at the park, head back to the city and maybe a quick stop at some of the many anime stores in town. Just keep the kids away from the adults-only section in some stores.

There is a great appreciation for Italian food in Kyoto and the kids swear that the best spaghetti ragu they have ever had was at Osteria Il Canto del Maggio. It was indeed amazing. The chef worked in Italy for 10 years before opening his own place in Kyoto.

If the weather is not great during your stay, there are plenty of family things to do. Several shopping streets are covered. There is a huge Pokemon store and a Sanrio store.

Also a trip to one of the entertainment arcades is fun but you might want to use earplugs as the sound level is intense. Bring a pouch or a fanny pack for each person; all the games take 100 yen coins and there are change machines on all floors of the arcades. Some of the games are fun to play in teams or against each other. There are always lots of Japanese kids there and young people on dates. The cinema is also fun with most movies also shown in English with Japanese subtitles and you can get fried chicken and boba tea as well as the traditional popcorn, sweet treats and drinks.

DAY 3 – ARWEN, 15

"I have known I wanted to move to Japan since I was 6 years old. I had been in Tokyo for about 30 minutes before I told my mom that I was going to live here one day. I can't say anything particular about why I love Japan, I just love everything there."

OUR ELDEST daughter preferred a Japanese-style breakfast to start the day: steamed rice, pickles, egg and cooked fish followed by a matcha latte. Most of the bigger hotels have the option of western-style or tradition Japanese breakfasts.

Gion is the beautiful old part of Kyoto that looks like it is a set from *Spirited Away*, one of the amazing Studio Ghibli movies we love (there are two Ghibli stores in Gion). Once you have wandered around Gion, you can walk about three kilometers to the cherry-tree-lined Philosopher's Path. Along the path is a highly regarded soba noodle counter called Juu-go, but you will have to reserve seats.

At the end of the Philosopher's Path is the start of a family friendly hike up the mountain Daimonji. The route takes 30 to 60 minutes depending on your pace and you will see many Japanese families making the hike to see the amazing view.

Try Tonkatsu, breaded cuts of pork, for dinner. There are many places at many price points to choose from but for a quick in-and-out dinner after an eventful day we enjoyed Katsukura Ginkaku-ji.

For an after-dinner experience try karaoke. You get your own room, you can dress up in costumes and perhaps the most fun of all is ordering drinks and snacks from a tablet.

Big Echo is one of the larger karaoke chains but we liked Vino Tagiri, which does not have private rooms but serves natural wines to sing along with.

If you have more time, Universal studios in Osaka is not too far and is great if you can be there when they open at 09:00 as this will give you a good three hours or so of very short queues. For a different day trip go to Nara deer park. It is large and beautiful and the deer roam freely in the park and are used to people and being fed. When you bow to the deer, they bow back.

Another great restaurant is the small French-style Le 14eme, where you choose your cut of meat and it is served with the best potatoes wedges. There is normally a chocolate mousse or a French butter cookie for dessert. Both are a must-try. The kids can have white or red grape juice and there is a small but amazing selection of natural wine for the parents.

| WORDS | NATE FRENCH & YUKI HATTA | TRANSLATION | RISA KAMIO |

TEMPLE CITY

Gathering places for centuries, temples and their gardens contain fabled treasures that are both spiritual and contemplative. From the most visited to lesser-known more serene locations. Let our experts be your guide.

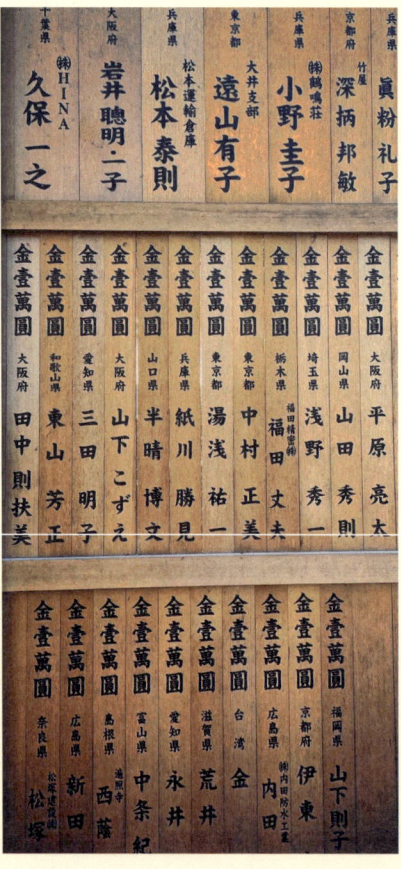

PHOTO: ICHI NAKAMURA, DITTE ISAGER

KIYOMIZU-DERA

ORIGINALLY built before Kyoto became the capital of Japan in the 8th century, the current structure was rebuilt in the 17th century without the use of a single nail. The complex sits at the top of Kiyomizu-zaka, a winding pedestrian street lined with traditional buildings and countless mochi shops. Be sure to check out Hōkan-ji Temple, though it is hard to miss as it towers over its neighboring buildings.

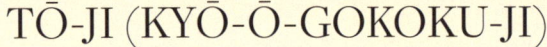

TŌ-JI (KYŌ-Ō-GOKOKU-JI)

ALMOST as old as Kiyomizu-dera located in the Minami Ward, Tō-ji (Kyō-ō-gokoku-ji) has an extensive pavilion and an imposing five-story pagoda that can be seen from afar. It also features the famous flea market Kōbō-san on the 21st of each month and another market, Garakuta-ichi on the first Monday of the month.

KYOTO GUIDE

PHOTO: ICHI NAKAMURA, MITSURU WAKABAYASHI, DITTE ISAGER, MINECHIKA ENDO

KENNIN-JI

DATING TO the 13th century, Kennin-ji is claimed to be the oldest Zen temple in Kyoto. The complex houses several grand halls with other smaller buildings, all adorned with intricate paintings and etchings.

KINKAKU-JI

THE TEMPLE of the Golden Pavilion, Kinkaku-ji was originally built in the 12th century for Shogun Ashikaga Yoshimitsu (who also had a Silver Pavilion known as Ginkaku-ji built, although the Silver Pavilion is not silver). After Yoshimitsu passed away, Kinkaku-ji was converted to a Zen temple and has been one of the most iconic sites of Kyoto ever since.

FUSHIMI INARI-TAISHA

KNOWN AS THE Torii Path, Fushimi Inari-taisha begins at the base of Inari Mountain and is a meandering 4-kilometer-long path with approximately 10,000 torii gates and smaller shrines dotted along the way.

TEMPLE PATHS LESS TAKEN

MIBU-DERA TEMPLE

A BUDDHIST TEMPLE of the Risshu sect, this was once the headquarters of the Shinsen-gumi, a special police force created in the late Edo period to protect the shogunate. The main hall has gorgeous wall paintings created by contemporary artists and a garden that is designated as a registered cultural property by Kyoto City. But Mibu-dera is all about the Mibu Kyogen performance in April and October. Mibu Kyogen, is an Important Intangible Folk Cultural Property and differs from ordinary Noh Kyogen in that it is performed silently, with all performers wearing masks and without using any dialogue to the accompaniment of instruments including gongs, drums, and flutes. Mibu Kyogen originated from the teachings of the Yuzu Nenbutsu Kyogen sect of Buddhism when monk Engaku Shonin adopted gestural pantomime as a means of preaching the teachings of Buddhism in the most easily understandable way in front of crowds. Mibu Kyogen has continued uninterrupted for approximately 700 years since 1300. Mibu Kyogen has no language barrier, so it is comprehensible for anyone interested in traditional Japanese performing arts.

PHOTO: TORU MIYAKI

SHŌGO-IN MONZEKI

THIS IS THE PRIMARY temple of the Buddhist Honzan Shugen sect and is most famous as a monzeki temple. Monzeki refers to specific temples where members of the imperial family and court nobles served as chief priests until the Meiji period. Shōgo-in is also the only temple to be designated twice as a temporary Imperial Palace due to fires at the palace during the Edo Period. Inside the temple, are 130 gorgeous wall paintings decorated with gold. Paintings of flowers and birds, sages, and the grandeur of nature were painted by the Kano school of art, an important style in the history of Japanese art. The paintings in Shōgo-in have been preserved in very good condition and the interior of the temple is entirely covered with paintings on goldleaf on sliding partitions, the subjects depicted in each room are different. Historically, guests would be guided to different rooms depending on the status of the visitor and purpose of the visit. This was Kyoto's unique way of hospitality by unfolding beauty for visitors.

In the fall of 2023, the shoin, or drawing room in Shōgo-in, will be reopened to the public after three years of restoration. The shoin was relocated from the Imperial Palace and the kato-mado (bell-shaped window) uses extravagant amounts of glass, which was extremely expensive in the early Edo period.

DAITOKU-JI

ONE OF THE MOST FAMOUS Zen temples in Kyoto, Daitoku-ji and its grounds were founded in the early 14th century by monk Sōhō Myōchō. In the mid-to-late 15th century, many of the buildings were destroyed by fire and after reconstruction, the importance of the temple really took off in the 16th century. At this time feudal lords (known as Sengoku daimyo) such as Oda Nobunaga and Toyotomi Hideyoshi were at the forefront of culture and were passionate practitioners of tea ceremonies. They enlisted tea master Sen no Rikyu to serve at the temple and continue to promote the importance of the tea ceremony. Additionally, Kanō Eitoku an important figure in the history of Japanese art and painting, and as one of the most prominent supporters of the Kanō School, was active at the temple. Daitoku-ji's influence on Japanese culture has continued as a gathering place for politicians, businesspeople, and top artists. It remains a hub where important sectors of society intersect.

OBAI-IN

A SMALLER TEMPLE within the Daitoku-ji complex, Obai-in was built by Oda Nobunaga in the mid-16th century for his father and was later renovated by Toyotomi Hideyoshi. Inside the temple, the beautiful moss and maple trees are a delight. Shrines and temples that are famous for autumn leaves are usually crowded during the tourist season and it can be difficult to view them, but Obai-in is a little-known spot and not so touristy. Obai-in has a particularly beautiful karesansui garden. These are dry gardens, or Zen gardens, made from stones and sand to represent mountains, rivers, and natural scenery. Obai-in also has the oldest surviving Zen Buddhist monastery. In the olden days, the most feared thing was fire, and throughout the precincts of Daitokuji, charms associated with water, such as dragons were painted on the ceiling and sculptures with water motifs were used in the architecture.

SABUTSU-TEI GARDEN

IN THE SABUTSU-TEI dry garden on the north side of Obai-in, a waterfall is made of standing stones and the water that flows from the waterfall turns into a stream with small boats floating and leads to the ocean of the hojo garden Hato-tei. This design is an interpretation of Zen which you must visit to feel it. In addition, the Jikichu-tei garden, said to have been built by tea master Sen no Rikyu when he was aged 66, has a particularly strong presence and is considered to be the highlight of Obai-in Temple. Sen no Rikyu was famous as a master of the tea ceremony, but he was a multi-faceted artist whoalso dedicated his time to architecture and garden design.

KORIN-IN TEMPLE

KORIN-IN is another smaller temple inside Daitoku-ji. Both the front gate (karamon) and the main hall to Korin-in are in the architectural style of the Muromachi period and both are important cultural properties. The main hall has an elegance that gives a sense of tranquility and calmness. Inside there is also a hojo garden restored by Kinsaku Nakane, the garden master who created the garden at the Adachi Museum of Art in Yasugi, which is said to be the best Japanese garden in the country. Because Daitoku-ji has such an extensive history with tea ceremony culture, all sub-temples in Daitoku-ji have tea rooms. Korin-in's tea room Kankyo-tei has a special structure with two entrances to a narrow space of about four tatami mats. The first is an entrance called nijiriguchi, a Sen no Rikyu creation that was built with the idea that everyone enters with heads lowered equally in front of the tea. The other tearoom in Korin-in is the kininguchi, which was created with political intentions by Furuta Oribe, a disciple of Sen no Rikyu, who said, "You can't make people of a high rank bow their heads," and therefore had taller entrances.

For Toryo Ito, the calm of nature and gardens can be linked with the inner composure of Zen.

TORYO ITO

Third-generation monk Toryo Ito explains that Kyoto isn't just about sights: it's about feelings and experiences. He shares two special places: Ryosokuin Temple in Gion, where he is deputy head priest, "offers a journey inside through Zen", and Shisendo in the Sakyo area "lets you appreciate nature's beauty." "Both places remind us to enjoy each moment. If you do, you will create lasting memories."

RYOSOKUIN TEMPLE

GION IS FAMOUS for its old streets and tea houses. Sometimes, you might see geishas walking here. In the heart of Gion is Ryosokuin Temple where visitors can learn about Zen meditation. Monks teach how to sit, breathe and focus. This Zen practice is more than relaxation, it's about understanding oneself and the world around. With Zen, you can feel connected to everything.

SHISENDO

JUST a 20-minute drive from Gion, you'll find Shisendo in the Sakyo district. This area is quieter and has a different charm. Shisendo's garden is a true work of art. Every plant and tree is cared for with love. When you walk, the Shishi-odoshi's gentle sound can be heard. It's a bamboo water tool that brings peace to your mind.

BEYOND KYOTO

Beaches, mountains and art lured intrepid noma explorers beyond Kyoto. Join waiter Miko Klages who, fueled by coffee, hiked, biked and swam, and caught trains, buses and ferries with fellow adventurers.

PHOTO: MIKO KLAGES

URADOME COAST

ONE WEEKEND we went to the Uradome Coast in Tottori Prefecture, a three-and-a-half-hour drive from Kyoto. This part of the west coast of Japan has a big surf culture, but regrettably we were unable to rent a board and wet suit no matter how hard we hustled, as the end of April was out of season. We settled for body surfing and an improvized rendition of French cricket played with a piece of driftwood and bouncy ball found in our accommodation. The Uradome Coast had hikes through steep coastal forests to hidden beaches and Tottori Prefecture is also noted for its sand dunes and is a tourist destination for many Japanese. It is also a big sake-brewing district, so it's a great region to visit for those wanting to visit some breweries.

ISHIGAKI

I HAVE SEEN some tiny airports in my life, but the Kansai Domestic Terminal is about the size of a shipping container. My predominantly pedantic European colleagues insisted on being unnecessarily early at the airport, reached by bus from Kyoto, and so we waited at the deserted gate longer than preferable for people who had drunk as many whiskey highballs as we had the night before.

Ishigaki is a small tropical island that is part of the Okinawa Prefecture and lies closer to Taiwan than it does to the Japanese mainland. A two-hour flight from Osaka, it's a whimsical little paradise that boasts white, sandy beaches, crystal-clear water, intricately shaped rock structures, abundant reefs and an array of weird and wonderful tropical fruit. The island has a population of less than 50,000 people and we rented an Airbnb on the north-western coast, an hour's drive from the airport in a pre-booked rental car. This villa lay 20 meters from a splendid private beach and became our haven for the following three days. Although we cooked every meal ourselves that weekend—something that seemed like a luxury after all the dining out back in Kyoto—we still experienced the epitome of Japanese hospitality in the form of our Airbnb host, who made us feel as though we were visiting our whacky aunt in a far-away land.

Being able to lie on a beach in the sunshine, play card games, read books and snorkel a reef abundant with sea life provided a compass of clarity and we frolicked through our days with a healthy, joyous mindset. On these trips I found the privilege of seclusion in pristine spots and Ishigaki was a prime example.

OSAKA

AN EASY day trip from Kyoto, Osaka is less than 30 minutes by train, and a city and surrounding metro area of nearly 20 million people. Osaka has plenty of charm but is raw and edgy, and certainly a change of pace from Kyoto. Notable sites to see are Osaka Castle and the colorful Dotonbori district. Near Dontonbori is Kuromon Ichiba Market, which winds along for 600 meters and dates to the Edo period. It's a major market for seafood but includes an array of other options too. The aquarium is an incredibly impressive structure—one of the largest in the world—and is located in a quiet seaside stretch of the Minato Ward. Not far from the aquarium is the Kyocera Dome, home to the Orix Buffalos, one of two local baseball teams in Osaka. Across the Yodo River, you can find the Hanshin Koshien Stadium, home to the Hanshin Tigers; the energy of any baseball game in Japan is intoxicating and electric and a great experience. Street-food stall Izakaya Toyo is in the Joto Ward and is a special experience, an izakaya with plenty of fire, bīru, and energy. When the sun sets, the digital art experience teamLab is a magical exhibition in the Nagai Botanical Garden. Osaka is a unique place, every bit as vibrant as its older sibling Tokyo, yet much closer to Kyoto and certainly easier to navigate.

Oyama Shrine, Kanazawa

KANAZAWA

A LITTLE MORE than two hours north on the JR Thunderbird 1 is Kanazawa, the capital of Ishikawa Prefecture on the Noto Peninsula. Sharing a coast with the Sea of Japan means a bounty of seafood that can be seen and purchased in the Ōmichō Market. One of Kanazawa's most notable attractions are the snow crabs fished off the coast. The magnificent Kanazawa Castle is adjacent to Kenroku-en Garden, a sprawling and meticulously manicured public garden regarded as one of the three great gardens in Japan. Kanazawa was spared the onslaught of allied air raids during World War II and has many beautifully preserved historical areas such as the Higashi Chaya District on the north side of the Asano River. A great coffee shop to visit is Townsfolk; for natural wine there is the cozy Ito Store; and if you can swing a reservation, a meal at Kataori along the Asano River is a one-in-a-lifetime experience, possibly one of the best restaurants in Japan.

NAOSHIMA

FOR A LONG weekend, or a few free days consider Naoshima, the art island in the Seto Inland Sea. Getting there takes a little over three hours. From Kyoto, take the Tokaido-Sanyo Shinkansen to Okayama. Change there for the local line to Uno Port, where you'll need to hop on a half-hour long ferry ride to the island. The area comprises three art sanctuaries on islands, Naoshima, Teshima, and the smallest of the three, Inujima. The island is quite small and a single road connects the ferry terminal on the west coast to the settlement on the eastern side. Riding a bike is by far the best way to see the island and it's best to plan ahead and reserve one with a motor. Make your first destination Akaito Coffee or Mikazukishoten for a boost of caffeine and check out the Naoshima Public Bath I Love You—it's a beautiful amalgamation of bygone decades of glamour and glitz, and is an art installation and actual bath house.

Naoshima has plenty of different galleries to visit as well as heaps of outdoor art, including the iconic Yayoi Kusama pumpkins. Some favorites that were visited were Chichu Art Museum, Lee Ufan Museum, Valley Gallery, Benesse House Museum, Hiroshi Sugimoto Gallery: Time Corridors and the Ando Museum. The beauty of these galleries is not confined to the art they contain; they are all small with focused exhibits that do not require all day to explore. It is possible to visit all in one day, but I would highly recommend spending extended time in Chichu, which we found simply stunning. The Art House Projects on the east coast of the island are also worth a visit, including, the Ando Museum, Art House Project: Minamidera, Art House Project: Gokaisho, Art House Project: Kinza, and Art House Project: Kadoya. The Naoshima Plan 2019 The Water is absolutely worth a visit, but is only open on Saturday and Sunday, so plan accordingly.

1

1. Yayoi Kusama's iconic *Yellow Pumpkin* on the south coast of Naoshima.

2. Hiroshi Sugimoto Gallery: *Time Corridors*.

3. Gokurakuji Temple Across from the Ando Museum, Naoshima

4. A view of the eastern port from Emperor Sutoku Shrine.

5. Inside the Valley Gallery by Tadao Ando.

TESHIMA

IF YOU ARE there on a Monday, catch a smaller local ferry from the main port of Naoshima for the one-hour ride to Teshima, a smaller, but equally beautiful art island. You can easily make a day trip out of Teshima, but there are options if you wish to stay overnight. It is best to rent a bike on arrival and ride to Teshima Art Museum, a single exhibition created by Rei Naito in collaboration with architect Ryue Nishizawa, which we found breathtaking and is sure to engage your imagination for at least a few hours. After that, head back towards the port and be nourished by a proper wood-fired pizza at Umi No restaurant. Thereafter, check out The Needle Factory and Teshima Yokoo House. Grab a coffee at the Teshima no Mado before catching the boat back to Naoshima. For more detailed information about all three art islands see the Benesse Art Site Naoshima website.

A small pizza truck sitting just above the Teshima Art Museum.

LAKE BIWA

WE SPENT a fair bit of time at Lake Biwa, a 45-minute train ride on the Tokaido-Sanyo line from Kyoto Station to Omi-Maiko Station on the west coast of the lake. Lake Biwa, in Shiga Prefecture, is the largest freshwater lake in Japan and is also one of the world's oldest, dating back at least 4 million years and home to the native Shijimi clam, a staple in many Japanese households. Biwa could easily be mistaken for a sea, given its enormity and white sandy beaches; we explored many beaches over numerous day trips to the lake and Omatsu-zaki was our favourite. A truly special place.

1. The river below Hozukyo Station.
2-7. Hiking Mt. Daimonji with the noma team.

PHOTO: TRACI PAGE MORRIS

KYOTO GUIDE

HIKING AROUND KYOTO

IT WASN'T all beaches and lakes. A hike that I'll never forget was Mount Atago. Starting at Arashiyama, the famous bamboo forest, the route traverses some of the most diverse mountain landscapes I experienced in Japan. Along most of the way, which is rather steep, a splendid view of Kyoto peeks through trees and shrubs. It's about four kilometers to the top, where the airy Atago-jinja Shrine awaits. On the way down, there is a fork in the path: to the left, you go back to your starting point; to the right, an even steeper decline that ends in up at a citrus plantation in a village called Sagamizuomiyanowakicho. By this time, you are exhausted and realise that although you're back in civilization, no bus is coming and you'll need to walk another hour down to Hozukyo JR Line Station to get back to Kyoto. Hozukyo Station happens to be one of the most surreal and beautiful train stations I have ever seen, perched on a high bridge over a beautiful river. On other occasions, we celebrated some colleagues' birthdays down by that river, barbecuing, swimming.

EVEN AFTER THREE months in Kyoto, having made time to integrate into city life, but also time for a handful of weekend trips away to explore, I certainly don't feel like I saw even nearly enough of the diversity that is Japan. There is just so much to see, even by means of the hyper-efficient Shinkansen railway system. Japan's landscapes are breathtaking and one could spend years exploring them.

12 WEEKS IN KYOTO

103 Creative individuals
5213 Guests
40 Opening days
Years of preparation
...and endless hours of dedication,
hard work and the love of what we do.

Clockwise from top left. Scenes from pre-opening week: Christine and René review decor options; final tasting before opening; Cornelia and Eri; front of house ready for service; well wishes from dear friends; testing lights with the front of house and the engineering team; Coady, Rebecca, Jun and Kenneth.

Clockwise from top left. René and Mees; Dining room post service; Afternoon briefing; Lea; Alisa, Annegret and Machiko in the afternoon sun; René and the BOH team; Mirek; Joseph, Carolyne, Machiko, Annegret, Max and Melissa pre-service; Risa, Sebastian and the Ace Engineering Dept.

Clockwise from top left. Miko; front of house afternoon briefing; Gaute, Kenneth, Alvaro, Rebecca and Jun; Office team Alisa, Neel, Risa and Nate; Kenneth, Walle and Nate; Pablo and Kenneth trimming bamboo; mis-en-place; Ben, Kenneth, Pablo and Rebecca; Coady, Jun, Mette, and Shui; Risa visiting a local Kyoto artisan.

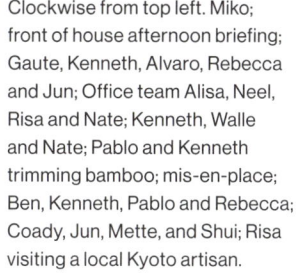

Clockwise from top left. Mees; Pablo, Kenneth, Rebecca and Ben; Pablo, Thomas, Kenneth, Misha, Mette, Mirek, Jun, and Coady; utensils after oiling; photo shoot of the menu with Ditte, Mette, and Jun; Mirek, Mette, Jun and Shui.

Clockwise from top left. Jun and an iris; Mees during the pre-opening dinner; Ben in a bed of flowers; Zdenka, Ali, and Tsubasa; Shanna and Arika during the pre-opening dinner; Coady, Toni, Pablo, Luca, Shui and Joe with the seaweed shabu-shabu.

NOMA IN KYOTO

From the final day of service: Clockwise from top left. Peter and Thomas during final briefing; Jun, Rebecca and Kevin; front of house team; Pablo and Jocelyn; Misha, Jun and Shui; Signing off the last ticket from the last service.

From the final day of service (cont): Clockwise from top left. René, Risa and Jun celebrating last call; back of house team; René taking in the moment; Risa signing the final service sheet; Matthias and Rebecca plating the final Ise-Ebi serving.

The Noma Kyoto team.

THANK YOU KYOTO

LILY COLLINS
ACTRESS

PHOTO: CHARLIE MCDOWELL

The rush of the bullet train
Flying by at every turn –
The astounding views of Mt. Fuji
The city's rich history, so vast,
so much to learn –

The buoyancy of the moss
The abundance of fresh air to breathe –
The elegance of the bamboo
Of towering heights we'd have
never believed –

The sea of umbrellas
The trickling of the rain –
The intense feelings and emotions
Too hard to properly explain –

The walks down Philosopher's Path
The divine soba noodles along
the way –
The cherry blossom explosions
bolder and brighter than words
can say –

The quiet of the temples
The calmness of the night –
When all the streets were empty
And the temperature just right –

The vibrancy of the markets
The crab sticks, fried desserts,
ice cream of every kind –
Little trinkets and miniatures
Hidden gems for all to find –

Savored meals of a lifetime
Tastes unlike any other –
Restaurants found down
winding paths
Patiently waiting to be discovered –

The picnics by the river
Complete with artisanal coffee
and delicately baked treats –
Enjoyed while perching on
patinaed stools
Far too beautiful to be seen
as merely just seats –

The cozy nights in our ryokan
Surrounded by decorative
rice paper screens –
Sitting cross-legged on the floor
Enjoying our tea ceremony,
complete with notes of roasted
black and matcha forest greens –

The mixing of customary textiles
And boldness of modern prints –
The innovative fashion for every age
Has stayed with us ever since –

It was a trip for the books
An experience to always hold dear –
Forever grateful for our time spent
in such a magical place
Where intention, respect,
and love felt ever so clear –

Thank you, Kyoto for your time,
Your memories, your heart –
For the wonderful humans we've met
who demonstrated to us that real
attention to detail
Is a way of life, a duty, a true art –

It's the embracing of the past
The acceptance of the now –
The anticipation of the future
so unique to you somehow –

that's allowed centuries of tradition
and antiquities to be preserved
for decades of travelers like ourselves
to visit and admire –
creating a world in which time
stands still
never ceasing to inspire –

We feel forever changed
Having been welcomed into
your home –
where your stove is always full,
hearth is always warm
and Mother Nature's untouched
earth meets humans' forged stone –

And no being,
no spirit,
no soul

ever feels alone.

THANKS TO THE SUPPLIERS OF NOMA KYOTO

TABLEWARE ARTISANS

Roberto Yuasa
Tokuhito Marukawa
Yoshiaki Tadaki
Kei Condo
Toru Hatta
Nobuhiko Tanaka
Nobue Ibaraki
Tetsuya Kobayashi
Asuka and Tenshin Juba
Noritaka Yamamoto
Kaori Uchida (Studio Knot)
Aya and Kazuhiro Tsubota
Saya Ueda
Keiko Murakami (sabi-nuno)
Jackie Iwami
Tomomi Kawakami
Tomomi Mizutani
Yoshihiro Funaki
Masaichi Ishida
Atsushi Ogata
Kiyoshi Eguchi (Kobosenta)
Ann-Charlotte Ohlsson
Hannah Blackall-Smith
Kristine Vedel Adeltoft
Mai Jørgensen
Janaki Larsen
Anne Mette Hjortshøj
Momoko Nakamura
Yuka Kurosu

SEAWEED EXPERT

Shogo Arai

ADDITIONAL DESIGN ELEMENTS

Aoni Textiles
Shuji Nakagawa
Reita Moriya

TATAMI

Mitsuru Yokoyama

NOREN

Samiro Yunoki
Masahiro Yamamoto (Shikisai)

KELP FOREST

Tenugui Kamawanu
Sea Vegetable
Natural Material Studio

FLOWERS

Hiroshi Nakamura

GARDEN LIGHTING

Ton Ton

BAMBOO

Hiroaki Nakagawa (Takemata)

WINE

Eishi & Mayuko Okamoto
Takahiko Soga
Keiichi Murakami
Bruce & Ryoko Gutlove
Atsushi Suzuki
Ken & Kazuko Sasaki
Atsuo Yamanaka
Yukiko & Kazuyuki Nakazawa
Yosuke Kondo
Kuwabara Kazuto
Hirotake Ooka
Tsuyoshi Kobayashi
Kenjiro & Mayumi Kagami

SAKE

Hidehiko Matsumoto
Kuniko Mukai
Masaru Terada
Philip Harper
Tomonari Miwa
Yasuhiko Niida
Hayato Shoji
Hiroaki Oku

BEER

Akio Kichise

WHISKY

Mitosaya Distillery
Yamatozakura Shuzo
Kanosuke
Ichiro
Mars
Akkeshi
Shizuoka

COFFEE

Weekenders

TEA

Tokuya Yamazaki (Kamo Nature Farm)
Kennichi Shizen Nouen
Organic Tea Farm Tukigase Kenkou Chaen Co.Ltd
Chiran Noen
Io (Yukiko and Simon)

INGREDIENTS

Manmatsu Seika
Kawaichi Shoten
Honest Farm
Yamaichi Suisan
Ishigaki Kosho-En
Takafumi Yoda
Terada Farm
Sea Vegetable
Fisherman's Wharf
Maruyata
SozoKobo
Shiraki Orchard
Maruken
Wakako Morihira
Kyoto Organic Action
Yasaiya
Moringa Farm
Nobuyasu Kawata
Shigetaka Fukunaga (a.k.a Bakabon-san)
Hanbey Fu
Kakusyo
Sumiya Bunjiro Shoten
Naeme
Temahima
Kawamura Suisan
Kobayashi Suisan
Kawaguchi Farm
Kaneshichi Shoten
Kato Miso
Shimuraya
Uchibori Jozo
Tofu Kobo Yuu
Matsushimaya
Yoshimura Farm
Togawa Poultry Farm
Osakaya Koji
Aisho
Midorinasu
Kamo-Tofu Kinki
Oomiya
Yumesanchi Tosayama
Farm Vegeco
Ome Farm
Agri Style
Suzuki Farm
Dot Science
Kawakyu
Hayashi Farm
Sontar Garden
Yasushi and Mariko Isozumi
Ohnishi Herb
Uoman Shoten
Aimono Kombu
Yagi Houchouten

NOMA DIRECTORY

551 Horai, 551horai.co.jp
10R Winery, 10rwinery.jp

A

Ace Hotel, acehotel.com
Ajidokoro, ajidocoro.jp
Akaito Coffee, akaitocoffee.net
Aoni Textiles, aoni.kyoto
Archi Coffee And Wine, @archi_kyoto
Arts & Science, arts-science.com
Arashiyama, kyoto-sagano.jp
Asahiyaki, asahiyaki.com
Ayanomimi, ayanomimi.com
Azuma Sushi, Honcho Nishi-iru Shomen-dori Higashiyama-ku, Kyoto

B

Bar K-Ya, 105 Yaoyacho, Nakagyo Ward, Kyoto, 604-8072
Bar Le Coq, bar-lecoq.info
Beau Paysage, 1334-5, Kurabara, Takane-cho, Hokuto-shi, Yamanashi
Beer Pub Takumiya, @beerpubtakumiya
Benesse Art Site Naoshima, benesse-artsite.jp
Berangkat, kyoto-berangkat.com
Big Echo karaoke, big-echo.jp
Bingo, @sake_nonki_bingo
Bistro Alpes,@winebar_alpes

C

Café/Bar Oil, FSS Building 6F, 442 Shirakabe-cho, Nakagyo-ku, Kyoto
Cantonese Restaurant Hosen, kantonhosen.wixsite.com/hosen
Cenci, cenci-kyoto.com
Chabuya, chabuya-honten.com
Chez Quasimodo, Takakura-dori NijoAgaru, Nakagyo-ku, Kyoto 604-0821
Chichi Kyoto, chichi.storeinfo.jp
Chrome, chrome-natural-winelife.com
Clamp Coffee Sarasa, &clampcoffeesarasa
Coyote, coyote-coffee.stores.jp
Craftman, craftman.owst.jp

D

Daitoku-ji Temple, daitokujidaijiin.com
Delta/Kyotographie, delta.kyotographie.jp
Demachi Futaba, 236 Seiryucho, Kamigyo Ward, Kyoto, 602-0822
Deux Cochons, 604-8214 Kyoto, Nakagyo Ward, Mukadeyacho, 372-3
Dig The Line Bottle & Bar, sakahachi.jp/digtheline-kyoto
Din Tai Fung, d.rt-c.co.jp/kyoto
Dogo Onsen, dogo.jp
Dotcomm, dot-comm.info
Dough, facebook.com/doughkt
Dupree, dupree.jp

E

Ebisugawa Gyoza Nakajima, nakajimagyoza.com
Essence, essencekyoto.com
Estre, @wine_beer_estre
Ethelvine, ethelvine.com

F

Farmoon Kyoto, @farmoon_kyoto
Flea Markets, howtojapan.net
Fushimi Inari Shrine, inari.jp

G

Gallery Utsuwakan, g-utsuwakan.com
Gear, bar-gear.biz
Ginkaku-ji, shokoku-ji.jp
Gion Rohan, 233 Nijuikkencho, Higashiyama Ward, Kyoto, 605-0077
Gion Manju, 196, Nakanocho, Higashiyama-ku Kyoto-shi, Kyoto, 605-0075
Gyoza ChaoChao, gyozakeikaku.com
Gyukatsu Kyoto Katsugyu – Kawaramachi, gyukatsu-kyotokatsugyu.com

H

Haaan!!, 287 Minamikurumayacho Nakagyo Ward Kyoto
Hachi Record Shop and Bar, @hachi_kyoto
Hanaré Machiya Guest Houses, hanare-kyoto.com
Hassenkaku, @8senkaqu
Hayakawa Hamonoten, hayakawa-hamonoten.com
Heian Antique Market, @heiannominoichi
Hieh Temple, hieizan.gr.jp
Hirakata Park, hirakatapark.co.jp
Hitomi, 96 Okikucho, Sakyo Ward, Kyoto, 606-8376
Hitsuji Doughnuts, 604-0092 Kyoto, Nakagyo Ward, Oicho, 355-1
Honke Daiichi-Asahi, honke-daiichiasahi.com
Hosoo, hosoo.co.jp
Hyotei, hyotei.co.jp

I

Ichimonjiya Wasuke, 69 Murasakino Imamiyacho, Kita-ku, Kyoto 603-8243
Ichiryu Manbai, 604-8031 Kyoto, Nakagyo Ward, Daikokucho, 71 World Hall 1st floor
Ichizawa, ichizawa.co.jp
Ikura Mokuzai, https://goo.gl/maps/i9gSDFyCLUyeVhid8
Ippodo Tea, global.ippodo-tea.co.jp
Iso Stand, isostand.isozumi.jp
Isshi Souden Nakamura, kyoto-nakamura.com
Ito Store, @110shoten
Izuu, www.izuu.jp

J

Jam +Sake Bar, @jamsakebar
Jikko, jikkocutlery.com
Jiki Miyazawa, jiki-miyazawa.com
Juu-go soba restaurant, @15_soba

K

Kaikado cafe, kaikado-cafe.jp
Kaikado, kaikado.jp
Kakizaki Shoten, @kakizakishoten
Kameya Kiyonaga, kameyakiyonaga.co.jp
Kanga-an, kangaan.jp
Karasemitei, r.goope.jp/karasemitei
Kashiyanona Wagashi, @kashiya.nona
Kataori, 3-36 Namikimachi, Kanazawa, Ishikawa 920-0928
Katsukura Ginkaku-ji, katsukura.jp/shops/ginkakuji
Katsukura Tonkatsu Sanjo Main Store, katsukura.jp/shops/sanjo
Kazariya, 96 Murasakino Imamiyacho, Kita Ward, Kyoto, 603-8243
Kazubar, 309-5 Bizenjimacho, Nakagyo Ward, Kyoto, 604-8023
Kenroku-en Garden, pref.ishikawa.jp/siro-niwa/kenrokuen
Kikunoi Honten, www.kikunoi.jp
Kinkaku-ji, shokoku-ji.jp
Kinobu, kinobu.co.jp
Kitano Tenmangu Shrine Street Market, kitanotenmangu.or.jp
Kiyomizu-dera Temple, kiyomizudera.or.jp
Kodai-ji Temple, kodaiji.com
Komorebino Natural Wine Bar, komorebino.com
Kumano Winehouse, @kwh_info
Kurasu, kurasu.kyoto
Kuromon Market, kuromon.com
Kurs, @curusu.kurs
Kyocera Museum, kyotocity-kyocera.museum
Kyoto Art Centre, kac.or.jp
Kyoto Brewing Co., kyotobrewing.com/
Kyoto Ceramic Centre, kyototoujikikaikan.kyoto
Kyoto Four Sisters Residence, foursisters-kyoto.com
Kyoto Issh ū Trail, kyoto-trail.net
Kyoto Kitcho Arashiyama, kyoto-kitcho.com/restaurant/arashiyama
Kyoto National Museum, kyohaku.go.jp
Kyoyasai, kyoyasai.kyoto

L

La Petite Cérine, facebook.com/LaPetiteCerine
La Pioche, facebook.com/2013lapioche
Le 14eme, @le_14e

Le Bouchon, bellecour.co.jp
Le Cabaret, @lecabaretinfo
L'escamoteur, @escamoteurbar
Lemon Stand, @lemon.stand.hiroshima
Lurra°, lurrakyoto.com

M

Maison de Frouge, ichigonoomise.com
Malebranche Kyoto, malebranche.co.jp
Mankamerou, mankamerou.com
Masutomi, masutomi.biz
Mibu Kyōgen, discoverkyoto.com/event-calendar/may/mibu-kyogen-mibu-dera
Mieri Shigemori, japanesegardens.jp
Mihana, @sumiyaki_mihana
Mikazukishoten, mikazukishoten.jp
Mitch Mitchell, 90-5 Shincho, Shimogyo Ward, Kyoto, 600-8001
Mitosaya Botanical Distillery, mitosaya.com
Miyako Hotel, global.miyakohotels.ne.jp
Miyamaso, miyamaso.org
Momoharu, 2nd floor, Taneike Building, 55 Tokiwagi-cho, Nakagyo-ku, Kyoto City
Monk, restaurant-monk.com

N

Nijo Aritsune, aritsune.jp

O

Ochaya Shigemori, ochaya.kyo2.jp
OEO Studio, oeo.dk
Ogata, 726 Shinkamanzacho, Shimogyo-ku, Kyoto
Okazuya Ishikawa, Japan, 221-2 Takakura-dori Shijosagaru Takazaimokucho, Kyoto 600-8082
Olive Concept, oliveconcept.com
Onikai, isozumi.jp/onikai
Oryori Menami, menami.jp
Osteria Il Canto del Maggio, italian-restaurant-1441.business.site
Ovgo Baker, ovgobaker.com

P

Passific Brewing, @passificbrewing
Pizzeria da Ciro, 75 Jodoji Nishidacho, Sakyo-ku, Kyoto, 606-8417
Pizzeria Napoletana Da Yuki, da-yuki.com
POJ Studio, pojstudio.com
Purple, purple-purple.com

R

R&Run Serviced Apartments, r-and-run.com
Rainmaker Kyoto, rainmaker-kyoto.com
Ramen Daiki, rs-daiki.moo.jp
Ramen Mugyu Vol. 2 Karasuma Takoyakushi, @ramen_mugyu
Ramen Nishiki, ramen-nishiki.com
Ramen Oyaji, 22 Hanazonokitsujiminamicho, Ukyo Ward, Kyoto, 616-8057
Ramen Touhichi, tousugu2020.thebase.in
Ritz Carlton, ritzcarlton.com

Robert Yellin Yakimono Gallery, japanesepottery.com
Rokuroku Dou, rokurokudo.jp
Ryosoku, ryosokuin.com

S

Sagra, sagra.jp
Sakaba Ikuramokuzai, facebook.com/yasuhiro.ikura
Sakai Shokai, sakai-shokai.jp
Sake Bar Yoramu, sakebar-yoramu.com
Salsiccia Deli, salsicciadeli.kinugoshi.net
Sambongi Shoten, sanbongi-shoten.com
Sanmikouan, sanmikouan.jp
Sanrio Gallery, sanrio.com
Sanze, @sanze_shimizu
Sanzen-in Temple, sanzenin.or.jp
Sea Vegetable, seaveges.com
Shisendo Temple, kyoto-shisendo.net
Shōgo-in Temple, shogoin.or.jp
Shokudou Ogawa, 204 Sendocho, Shimogyo Ward, Kyoto, 600-8019
Shokudo Miyazaki, 188 Sendōchō, Shimogyo Ward, Kyoto, 600-8019
Shuji Nakagawa, nakagawa.works
Slō Kyoto, @slo.kyoto
Slow Cave, wineshopslowcave.com
Sobatsuru, sobatsuru.com
Soif Hokuto, soif.jp
Sokyo Gallery, gallery-sokyo.jp
So San, @pilgrimsosan
Soujiki Nakahigashi, soujiki-nakahigashi.co.jp
Suba Soba, @subasoba
Sugari, sugari.net
Style Coffee, stylecoffee.jp
Sushi Sakai, 92 Nishiuoyacho, Nakagyo Ward, Kyoto, 604-8142
Sushi Saeki, 663 Izumicho, Nakagyo Ward, Kyoto, 604-0015
Sushi Suzuka, 305 Nakagyo Ward, Forum Eikawa 1F, 604 - 0966
Switch Coffee Tokyo, switchcoffeetokyo.com

T

Tadka2, tadka-kyoto.com
Tagiri, @tagiri_kyoto
Taiho, 149 Nishinokyo Hoshigaikecho, Nakagyo-ku, Kyoto
Takamura, japaneseknives.eu
Tarel, @tarel_kyoto
Tawaraya Ryokan, 278 Nakahakusancho, Nakagyo Ward, Kyoto, 604-8094
Tearoom Toka, tokaseisei.com
Tempura Matsu, 21-26 Umezu Onawabacho, Ukyo Ward, Kyoto, 615-0925
Tenryuji, tenryuji.com
Terada Honke, teradahonke.co.jp
Terasaki Coffee, terasakicoffee.com
Teshina no Mado, teshimanomado.com
Teuchisoba Kanei, 11-1 Murasakino Higashifujinomoricho, Kita-ku, Kyoto, 603-8223
Tōfuku-ji, discoverkyoto.com
To. Izakaya, https://www.fudokyoto.com/to/
To-ji Temple, toji.or.jp
Tokusa, @tokusa_sapporo

Tominokoji Yamagishi, tominokoji-yamagishi.com
Tonkatsu Ichiban, tonkatsuichiban.com
Tousuiro, tousuiro.com
Townsfolk Coffee, townsfolkcoffee.shop
Tsukemono, traditionalkyoto.com/eat/pickles
Tsukigase Organic Tea Farm, tukicha.com
Tsukiji Aritsugu, aritsuguknives.com
Tsuki no Tofu, Chiba Pref. Katorigunkouzakimachi Kouzakihonjuku 2055
Tsuneya Densuke, 84 Kannoncho, Nakagyo-ku, Kyoto, 604-0821

U

Ueda Liquor Store, 7 Yamabanakawaharacho, Sakyo Ward, Kyoto, 606-8003, Japan
Ukai Shoten, Kyoto-shi, Kamigyo-ku, Omiya-dori, Teranouchi-agaru, 3 Chome
Umi no Restaurant, il-grano.jp/umi

V

Vana Vasa, @vanavasa_kamakura
Vegan Ramen Uzu, vegan-uzu.com
Vino Tagiri, @tagiri_kyoto
Vou, voukyoto.com

W

Weekenders Coffee, weekenderscoffee.com

X

Xuemeihua Saikontan, kiwa-group.co.jp/xeumeihua_saikontan

Y

Yagihouchou, yagihouchou.theshop.jp
Yakitori Kaminari, 20-1 Mibuaiaicho, Nakagyo Ward, Kyoto, 604-8812
Yakitori Nishino, 36-16 Saiinkitayakakecho, Ukyo Ward, Kyoto, 615-0026
Yamahon, gallery-yamahon.com
Yanagi Koji Taka, taka-kyoto-japan.net
Yorocco Beer, yorocco-beer.com
Yoshida Farm, @yoshida_dairy_farm
Yoshihiro Funaki, facebook.com/people/Yoshihiro-Funaki
Yudofu Sagano, 45 Saga Tenryuji Susukinobaba-cho, Ukyo-ku, Kyoto 616-8385
Yukifuran Sato, 102 Higashiiri Yaohira Building, Shinbashi-dori Hanamikoji, Higashiyama-ku, Kyoto-shi

Z

Zero Waste Kyoto, zerowaste.kyoto

The final expeditor sheet of Noma Kyoto.

PHOTO: FRITZ BUZIEK